Gooseberry Patch

Christmas COOKIES

A collection of incredibly edible cookies,
plus nifty packaging & cookie swap how-to's!

Gooseberry Patch

An imprint of Globe Pequot
246 Goose Lane
Guilford, CT 06437

www.gooseberrypatch.com

1•800•854•6673

Copyright 2019, Gooseberry Patch 978-1-62093-332-9

Photo Edition is a major revision of *Christmas Cookies.*

Do you have a tried & true recipe...

tip, craft or memory that you'd like to see featured in a **Gooseberry Patch** cookbook? Visit our website at **www.gooseberrypatch.com** and follow the easy steps to submit your favorite family recipe. Or send them to us at:

Gooseberry Patch
PO Box 812
Columbus, OH 43216-0812

Don't forget to include the number of servings your recipe makes, plus your name, address, phone number and email address. If we select your recipe, your name will appear right along with it... and you'll receive a **FREE** copy of the book!

Table of
CONTENTS

Come to a COOKIE EXCHANGE

What's a cookie exchange?

It's a simple, quick & easy way for friends & family to swap sweet treats. Arrive with a few dozen of your favorite goodies and leave with a candy-box assortment!

And the treats don't have to be home-baked. Try exchanging layered mixes, candy, chocolate-dipped pretzels, popcorn balls, savory snack mixes or mulled cider and cocoa mixes.

With just a few simple party basics, you'll be ready to hold a cookie swap of your own...it's so easy!

Dedication:

For the kid in all of us...who can't stop at just one cookie!

Appreciation:

Thank you, friends, for sharing your cherished cookie recipes...every one's a keeper!

PLANNING...
Deck the halls, walls & mantels!

Make a special CD music mix of all-time favorites, or you can set your CD player to shuffle for a variety of very merry music.

Find a roomy table for everyone to place their cookies on when they arrive. Be sure to move chairs away from the table so everyone can easily collect their goodies.

Make tags (we've given you lots of clever ideas!) for all the goodies that will be arriving. Then, everyone will know what treat they're collecting (or sampling)!

Jot down a shopping list of anything you'll want for the party...spiced cider, eggnog, cocoa or punch. Would you like to have a few appetizers for friends to enjoy while chatting?

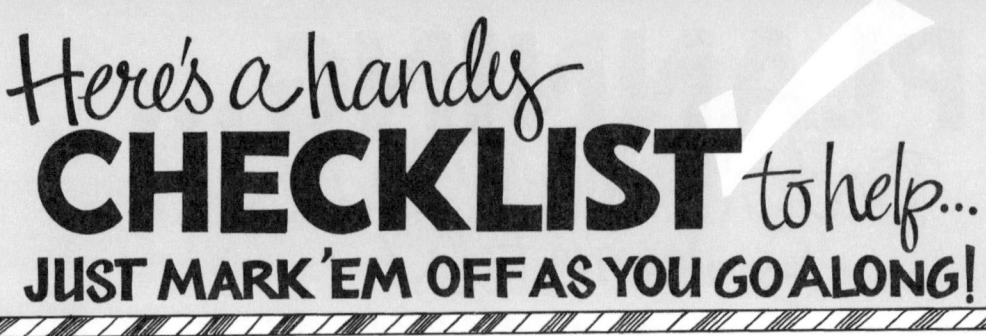

Here's a handy CHECKLIST to help...

JUST MARK 'EM OFF AS YOU GO ALONG!

1 — Choose a date & time for your get-together.

2 — Mail invitations to 6 or 8 friends (so everyone gets a nice assortment of goodies)! Recipe cards make charming invitations or use pretty ribbon to tie a note to a tin cookie cutter. For invites in a jiffy, just copy, cut & color the ones we've provided!

3 — Let friends know how many dozen cookies to bring. It's easy...one dozen for each person coming to the swap.

4 — Bake your goodies!

Now...ready, set, relax! It's all about having fun and making memories with family & friends.

Frost-Kissed
CUT-OUTS

Nana's Old-Fashioned Sugar Cookies

Ginnie Wible
McMurray, PA

*I sprinkle these with fine, colored sugars…there's no need
for frosting with their wonderful flavor!*

1 c. butter, softened
1 c. sugar
2 eggs, beaten
2 t. vanilla extract
1 c. sour cream
5 c. all-purpose flour

2 t. baking powder
1 t. baking soda
1-1/4 t. salt
1 T. nutmeg
Garnish: fine, colored sugars

Blend butter and sugar until fluffy; set aside. Stir together eggs, vanilla and sour cream; mix well and set aside. Combine flour, baking powder, baking soda, salt and nutmeg. Add flour mixture alternately with egg mixture to the butter mixture; blend well. Chill in refrigerator overnight. Roll out dough, a softball-size amount at a time, on a floured surface with a floured rolling pin. Roll out to 1/16 to 1/8-inch thickness; cut with cookie cutters. Arrange on ungreased baking sheets; sprinkle as desired with colored sugars. Bake at 375 degrees for 5 to 7 minutes, until golden. Cool on a wire rack; store loosely covered. Makes 7 to 8 dozen.

Think what a better world it would be if we all, the whole world, had cookies and milk about three o'clock every afternoon and then lay down on our blankets for a nap.
–Robert Fulghum

Frost-Kissed **CUT-OUTS**

Dusen Confectos

Ellie Grisham
Whitewater, WI

These cookies are nice to make with a friend, sister, mom or even the kids...one person can spread jam while the other rolls them in sugar.

2 c. butter, softened	1/4 t. salt
1 c. sugar	1/2 lb. almonds, ground
1 t. vanilla extract	12-oz. jar raspberry jam
3-1/4 c. all-purpose flour	Garnish: sugar

Blend together butter and sugar. Add vanilla; stir well. Stir in flour, salt and almonds. Roll dough out 1/8-inch thick and cut into an even number of matching shapes; arrange on ungreased baking sheets. Bake at 350 degrees for 8 minutes. Spread half the cookies with a thin layer of raspberry jam, reserving the rest for another recipe; top with remaining cookies. Roll in sugar. Let cool on rack. Makes 4 to 5 dozen.

Retro lunchboxes can be found in such terrific colors and patterns, and they make fun gift boxes for sharing cookies!

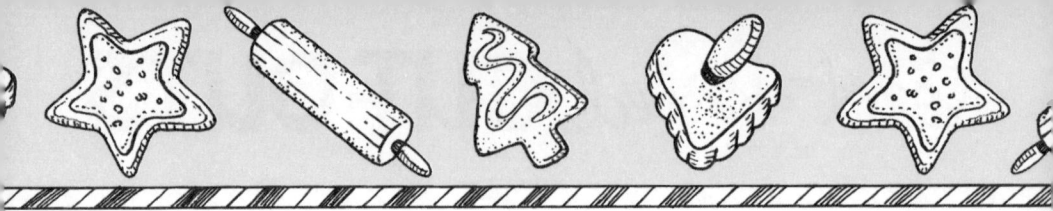

Butterscotch Gingerbread

Kathy Eichhorn
Richmond Hill, GA

*This is my mother's recipe and it's my favorite holiday cookie
in both fall and winter...the kids love it too!*

1/2 c. butter, softened
1/2 c. brown sugar, packed
3.4-oz. pkg. cook & serve
    butterscotch pudding mix
1 egg, beaten
1-1/2 c. all-purpose flour

1/2 t. baking soda
1-1/2 t. ground ginger
1 t. cinnamon
Optional: frosting,
    colored sugars

Blend together butter, brown sugar and pudding; mix well. Beat in
egg; stir in remaining ingredients. Chill until slightly firm; roll out
dough to 1/4 to 1/2-inch thickness and cut into shapes. Arrange on
a greased baking sheet and bake at 350 degrees for 10 to 12 minutes.
Decorate as desired. Makes one to 2 dozen.

Mock Whipped Cream Frosting

Brenda Doak
Delaware, OH

Add your favorite food coloring if you like.

1 c. milk
2 T. all-purpose flour
1 c. sugar

1 c. butter
1 t. vanilla extract

Combine milk and flour in a saucepan; cook over medium heat until
thickened. Chill. Blend sugar, butter and vanilla in a bowl. Add milk
mixture; beat with an electric mixer until whipped. Makes about
3 cups.

Frost-Kissed **CUT-OUTS**

Cookies for Santa

Leslie Stimel
Clayton, NC

Don't forget these on Christmas Eve!

2/3 c. butter
3/4 c. sugar
1 T. plus 1 t. milk
1 t. vanilla extract

1 egg
2 c. plus 2 T. all-purpose flour
1-1/2 t. baking powder
1/4 t. salt

Blend butter, sugar and milk with an electric mixer on medium speed. Add vanilla and egg; beat well. Add flour, baking powder and salt; mix to combine. Roll out to 1/4-inch thickness and cut with cookie cutters; arrange on ungreased baking sheets and bake at 375 degrees for 7 to 9 minutes. Makes about 2-1/2 dozen.

Send friends & family holiday cards with a little something extra inside...a cookie cutter and favorite recipe. What a sweet surprise!

Fancy Puff Cookies

Lisa McCain
Bartlett, NE

*There's a yummy cream-cheese filling between these
sandwich cookies.*

2 c. all-purpose flour
1 c. butter, softened
1/2 t. salt
1-1/2 T. half-and-half

1 T. cold water
1 egg white, beaten
Garnish: white and
   colored sugars

Add flour to a large bowl; cut in butter with a fork or pastry cutter
until well blended. Combine salt, half-and-half and water; add to
flour mixture and stir until liquid is just absorbed. Cover and chill for
one hour. Divide into 2 portions; roll out 1/4-inch thick on a floured
surface. Cut out with a 1-1/2 inch round cutter; arrange on ungreased
baking sheets. Brush with beaten egg white; sprinkle half with white
sugar and half with colored sugar. Bake at 350 degrees for 5 to 8
minutes, just until golden. Let cool; spread white sugar cookies with
filling and top with colored sugar cookies. Makes 2 to 3 dozen.

Filling:

1 c. powdered sugar
1/2 c. butter, softened

1 T. cream cheese, softened
1 t. vanilla extract

Combine all ingredients; mix until creamy.

Turn Christmas treats
into sweetly wrapped
treasures...use pretty papers,
handcrafted tags and
cheery red & white ribbons.

Frost-Kissed CUT-OUTS

White Velvet Cut-Outs

Dawn Gorenschek
Van Dyne, WI

These are by far the best sugar cookies I've ever had!

2 c. butter, softened
8-oz. pkg. cream cheese,
    softened
2 c. sugar

2 egg yolks, beaten
1 t. vanilla extract
4-1/2 c. all-purpose flour
Optional: candy sprinkles

Blend together butter and cream cheese; add sugar, egg yolks and vanilla. Gradually add flour. Chill for 2 hours; roll out on a floured surface to 1/4-inch thickness. Cut into desired shapes; place on greased baking sheets and bake at 350 degrees for 10 to 12 minutes. Let cool completely and frost; top with sprinkles, if desired.
Makes 7 dozen.

Frosting:

3-1/2 c. powdered sugar,
    divided
3 T. butter
1 T. shortening

1/2 t. vanilla extract
1/4 c. milk
Optional: food coloring

Combine 1-1/2 cups sugar, butter, shortening, vanilla and milk; beat until smooth. Add remaining sugar and food coloring, if desired; beat with an electric mixer on medium speed for 3 minutes until creamy.

Keep your soft cut-outs soft by adding one or 2 apple quarters to the cookie jar...just remove the apples in 2 days.

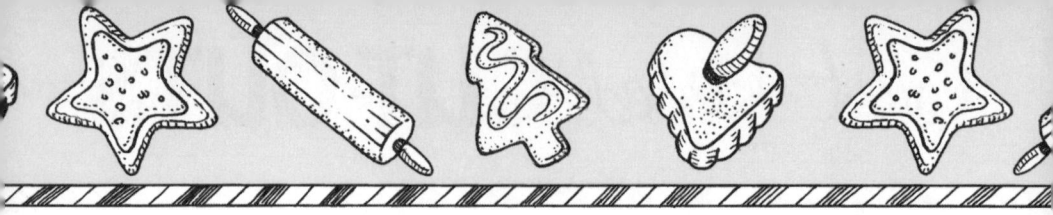

Knapp Kuchen

Rene Gusterson
Oakland, NJ

This was my Great Aunt Marge's recipe. Her cookie cutters and recipes were handed down to me when I got married, and I use them every winter to make these cookies with my daughter, Jenna.

1/2 c. butter, softened
1 c. sugar

5 eggs, beaten
4 c. all-purpose flour

Blend together butter and sugar in a medium bowl; set aside. Combine eggs and flour in a separate bowl; mix well. Add to butter mixture and mix to a dough consistency. Roll out to 1/4-inch thickness and cut with cookie cutters; arrange on greased baking sheets. Bake at 325 degrees for 12 to 15 minutes. Let cool completely and decorate as desired. Makes 5 to 6 dozen.

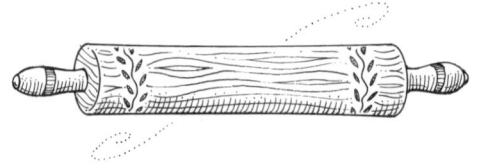

Caramel Icing

Karen Stoner
Delaware, OH

This icing works for topping cake, brownies, cookies...even ice cream!

1 c. buttermilk
1 c. butter, softened
1 t. baking soda

2 c. sugar
1 t. vanilla extract

Mix all ingredients together except vanilla in a saucepan over medium heat. Stir mixture until it reaches the soft-ball stage, or 234 to 243 degrees on a candy thermometer. Remove from heat; add vanilla. Beat until mixture turns a caramel color and is thick enough to spread. Makes about 4 cups.

Crofani

Carol Vickers
New Philadelphia, OH

When my mother came from Italy she brought many warm memories, wonderful stories and treasured traditions. This recipe for pastry was her grandmother's and something she fondly remembered.

2 c. all-purpose flour
2 t. baking powder
3 T. sugar
2 eggs, beaten

3 T. butter, softened
1/2 to 3/4 c. milk
oil for frying
Garnish: powdered sugar

Sift flour, baking powder and sugar together; add eggs and butter a little at a time. Stir in milk a little at a time until mixture is the consistency of pie dough; knead well. Roll out dough to 1/4-inch thickness on a floured surface. Cut into 2"x1" squares or cut with cookie cutters as desired. Heat 1 to 2 inches oil in a skillet over medium-high heat; drop in dough pieces and fry, a few at a time, until puffy and lightly golden. Remove with a slotted spoon; drain on paper towels. Sprinkle with powdered sugar when cool. Store in an airtight container. Makes about 10 dozen.

A recipe for cheer! Cover a cardboard recipe box with colorful paper using spray adhesive. Wrap cookies in tissue paper and tuck inside. Don't forget to jot down the cookie recipe on a recipe card and tie to the box with a pretty ribbon.

Orange-You-Glad Cookies

Jackie Balla
Walbridge, OH

I get requests for this cookie recipe all the time!

1 c. butter, softened
1 c. sugar
1 egg, beaten
2-1/2 c. all-purpose flour

1 t. baking powder
2 T. orange juice
1 T. vanilla extract

Combine butter, sugar and egg in a large mixing bowl; beat with an electric mixer on medium speed until creamy, about one to 2 minutes. Add flour, baking powder, orange juice and vanilla; continue mixing an additional one to 2 minutes. Cover and chill for 2 to 3 hours until dough is firm. Roll dough to 1/4-inch thickness and cut into shapes with cookie cutters. Place one inch apart on lightly greased baking sheets. Bake at 350 degrees for 6 to 10 minutes until edges are lightly golden. Cool and frost. Makes 2 dozen.

Frosting:

3 c. powdered sugar
1/3 c. butter, softened
1 t. vanilla extract

1 to 2 T. orange juice
Optional: red and yellow
    food coloring

Combine all ingredients; beat until fluffy.

Nestle bite-size cookies inside a teacup...what a thoughtful gift.

Frost-Kissed CUT-OUTS

Spicy Ginger Cookies

Rebecca Chrisman
Citrus Heights, CA

To save time during the holidays, I prepare this cookie dough about 3 months ahead of time and freeze it.

3 c. all-purpose flour
1 t. baking soda
1/4 t. salt
2 t. ground ginger
1 t. cinnamon
1/2 t. nutmeg
1/4 t. ground cloves

3/4 c. shortening
3/4 c. brown sugar, packed
1/2 c. molasses
1 egg, beaten
Garnish: frosting, colored sugar,
    candy sprinkles, raisins

Combine flour, baking soda, salt and spices; set aside. Blend together shortening and brown sugar until light and fluffy; beat in molasses and egg. Stir in flour mixture just until combined. Refrigerate at least 2 hours or overnight. Divide dough into 4 portions; roll out each portion 1/4-inch thick on a floured surface. Flour cookie cutters and cut into desired shapes. Arrange on greased baking sheets; bake at 350 degrees for 10 to 12 minutes. Let cool on wire racks. Frost and decorate as desired. Makes 4 dozen.

Make a frost-kissed snowman! Ice 3 round cut-out cookies with white icing, then arrange on a plate to resemble a snowman. Add colorful candies for a cheery face and buttons, then tie on a licorice whip scarf and add a gumdrop hat. The kids will love him!

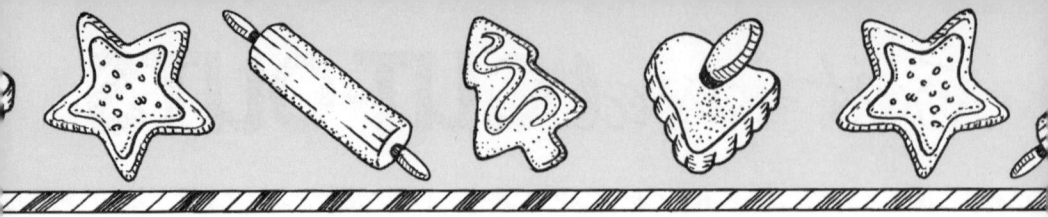

Chocolate Cut-Outs

Nancy Cavagnaro
Mountain View, CA

You'll have a hard time eating just one!

1 egg, beaten
2/3 c. butter, softened
3/4 c. sugar
1 t. vanilla extract
1/4 c. baking cocoa

1-1/2 c. all-purpose flour
1 t. baking powder
1/2 t. salt
Optional: frosting, colored sugar

Combine egg, butter and sugar; blend until creamy. Add remaining ingredients. Form dough into 2 flattened rounds; chill. Roll out on a floured surface to 1/8-inch thickness. Cut with cookie cutters as desired; place on ungreased baking sheets. Bake at 350 degrees for 8 to 10 minutes. Let cool; frost and sprinkle with sugar, if desired. Makes 2 to 3 dozen.

Peanut Butter Frosting

Kendall Hale
Lynn, MA

Try this paired with Chocolate Cut-Outs for a delicious taste.

1/2 c. creamy peanut butter
5 T. margarine, softened

1 c. powdered sugar
Optional: 1 to 3 T. milk

Beat peanut butter and margarine with an electric mixer on medium speed. Add sugar; beat to desired consistency. Add milk if too thick. Makes about 2 cups.

No time to frost Chocolate Cut-Outs?
Just top with a stencil and gently dust with
powdered sugar or glittery sanding sugar...beautiful!

Frost-kissed **CUT-OUTS**

Best-Ever Sugar Cookies

April Gadoury
Coventry, RI

A soft sugar cookie with a hint of maple flavor!

1-1/4 c. sugar
1 c. butter, softened
2 eggs, beaten
1/4 c. maple-flavored syrup
1 T. vanilla extract
3-1/2 c. all-purpose flour,
   divided

3/4 t. baking powder
1/2 t. baking soda
1/2 t. salt
Optional: candy sprinkles,
   chopped nuts,
   mini semi-sweet
   chocolate chips, frosting

Combine sugar and butter in a large bowl. Beat with an electric mixer on medium speed until well blended. Add eggs, syrup and vanilla; mix well and set aside. Combine 3 cups flour, baking powder, baking soda and salt; beat into sugar mixture gradually on low speed. Mix until well blended; divide into 4 portions. Wrap with plastic wrap and refrigerate for one hour to overnight. Sprinkle one tablespoon remaining flour onto a length of wax paper; place one dough portion on top. Flatten slightly; turn over, add more flour and another length of wax paper. Roll dough to 1/4-inch thickness; cut out with floured cookie cutters. Place 2 inches apart on ungreased baking sheets. Decorate as desired with sprinkles, nuts or chocolate chips, or leave plain to be frosted later. Bake at 375 degrees for 5 to 9 minutes. Makes 3 to 4 dozen.

*Whoever heard of a regular home
without a cookie jar?
'twould be a drab situation indeed.*
-Alice M. Child

Cocoa-Almond Cut-Outs

Vickie
Gooseberry Patch

Chopped almonds add a nutty crunch to these cut-out cookies.

3/4 c. butter, softened
14-oz. can sweetened
   condensed milk
2 eggs
1 t. vanilla extract
1/2 t. almond extract

2-3/4 c. all-purpose flour
2/3 c. baking cocoa
2 t. baking powder
1/2 t. baking soda
1/2 c. chopped almonds

Combine butter, condensed milk, eggs, vanilla and almond extract in a large mixing bowl; mix well and set aside. Combine flour, cocoa, baking powder and baking soda; gradually add to butter mixture until well blended. Stir in almonds. Divide dough into 4 portions; wrap each in plastic wrap and flatten into a disk. Chill for 2 hours; remove each portion when ready to roll out. Roll out on a floured surface to about 1/8-inch thickness. Cut into desired shapes. Arrange on lightly greased baking sheets and bake at 350 degrees for 6 to 8 minutes. Cool completely on wire racks. Makes 6 dozen.

Keep an eye out at flea markets and tag sales for vintage silver spoons to tie onto jars of homemade cocoa mix.

Frost-Kissed CUT-OUTS

Herbed Sugar Cookies

Kathy Grashoff
Fort Wayne, IN

Wrap these up and give to your favorite gardening friend.

1 c. butter, softened
1-1/4 c. sugar
1 egg, beaten
2-2/3 c. all-purpose flour

1/2 t. salt
2 T. fresh thyme, chopped
2 T. fresh rosemary, chopped

Beat butter with an electric mixer on medium speed until creamy; gradually add sugar, beating well. Blend in egg; set aside. Combine flour and salt; add to butter mixture, beating at low speed until blended. Stir in herbs. Divide dough into 4 portions; roll each portion to a 1/4-inch thickness on a lightly floured surface. Cut dough with assorted tree-shaped cookie cutters; arrange on ungreased baking sheets. Bake at 350 degrees for 8 to 10 minutes or until lightly golden. Let cool one minute on sheets. Remove to wire racks to cool completely. Makes 3 to 4 dozen.

Layers of sweetness...fill an aluminum canister, available at craft stores, with a stack of round cookies. Twist on the lid, wrap with ribbon, tie on a jingle bell and a tag. A gift in a jiffy!

Christmas Sugar Hands

Georell Bracelin
Bend, OR

My brothers and I looked forward to these cookies every year. One by one we would place our hands on the dough while my mother traced around our fingers. Then we would carefully arrange the cookies on tin sheets and watch them bake in the oven. We would frost them ourselves, creating rings, watches and painted fingernails on our very own sugar "hands."

1 c. shortening
1 c. sugar
2 eggs, beaten
1-1/2 t. vanilla extract

2-1/2 c. all-purpose flour
1-1/2 t. baking powder
Optional: 1/2 t. salt
Garnish: frosting

Mix together shortening and sugar; stir in eggs and vanilla. Add dry ingredients; mix well. Chill in refrigerator for at least one hour to overnight. Roll out on a floured surface to 1/4-inch thickness; gently place hands on dough and trace with a butter knife. Arrange on ungreased baking sheets. Bake for 10 minutes at 350 degrees. Let cool on wire racks; frost as desired. Makes 2 to 3 dozen.

Butter versus margarine...butter always gives cookies a richer flavor. Margarine will work for baking, but be sure to avoid low-fat, liquid and soft spreads.

Sand Tarts

Shelley Berrier
Belleville, PA

Knowing how much my dad loves these cookies, I can't let a
Christmas go by without baking him some Sand Tarts!

1-1/4 c. margarine, softened
2 c. sugar
2 eggs, beaten
4 c. all-purpose flour
powdered sugar
1 to 2 egg whites, beaten
Garnish: colored sugar,
   walnut halves

Blend together margarine and sugar; stir in eggs. Add flour and mix
well. If necessary, add more flour so that dough is not sticky. Roll out
dough as thinly as possible on a surface sprinkled with powdered
sugar. Cut out as desired with cookie cutters. Place on ungreased
baking sheets; brush each cookie with egg white and sprinkle with
colored sugar. Press a walnut half onto each cookie. Bake at
350 degrees for 4 minutes on bottom oven rack; move to top oven
rack and bake an additional 4 minutes. Watch carefully to avoid
burning. Makes 8 to 10 dozen.

Be original...fill a Chinese take-out box
with homemade cookies for gift-giving!

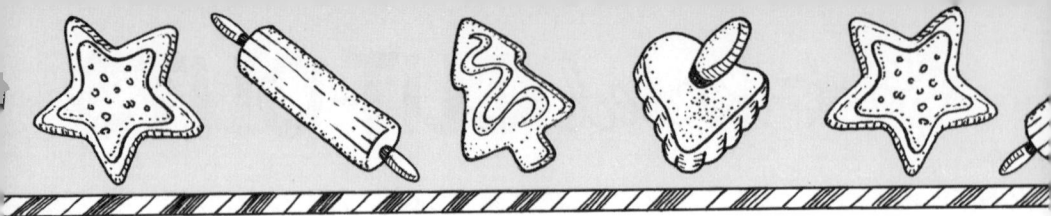

Icebox Cookies

Barbara Martin
Menominee, MI

When my mother and I made these cookies, she would bake and I would decorate. Many of the cookies were given to family & friends and I felt proud to know someone else got to enjoy my masterpieces!

3/4 c. butter, softened
3/4 c. shortening
1 c. sugar
1 c. brown sugar, packed
3 eggs, beaten
1 t. vanilla extract
2 t. baking soda

1/2 c. water
4 c. all-purpose flour
1 t. salt
1 t. cinnamon
Optional: 3/4 c. finely chopped
    nuts, frosting

Blend together butter, shortening and sugars. Add eggs and vanilla; add nuts if using. Mix well and set aside. Stir baking soda into water; set aside. Mix dry ingredients; stir into butter mixture, alternating with baking soda mixture. Dough will be soft and sticky. Freeze dough for 24 hours. Roll out small amounts of chilled dough on a floured surface 1/4-inch thick; cut with cookie cutters. Arrange on greased baking sheets; bake for 8 to 10 minutes at 350 degrees. Frost as desired. Makes 5 to 6 dozen.

FOR YOU!

Fill each cup of an old-fashioned muffin tin with a different type of cookie...what a tasty sampler!

Holiday Butter Cookies

Debi DeVore
Dover, OH

These will be one of your most-asked-for recipes.
So simple and delicious.

2 c. butter, softened
2 c. powdered sugar
4 eggs, beaten
1 t. baking soda

1 t. lemon juice
1 T. milk
5-1/2 c. all-purpose flour

Blend together butter, powdered sugar and eggs in a large mixing bowl; set aside. Dissolve baking soda in lemon juice; add to butter mixture. Stir in milk and flour gradually. Roll dough to 1/4-inch thickness and cut with cookie cutters. Arrange on ungreased baking sheets; bake at 350 degrees for 8 minutes. Makes 6 to 7 dozen.

Warm cookies dipped in cold milk...one of life's simple pleasures.

-Unknown

Kolacky

Barbara Ann Rouse
Reseda, CA

Kolacky is a Polish pastry my grandmother made. My job was making the thumbprint, and to be the first one to taste the Kolacky just out of the oven.

1-1/2 c. all-purpose flour
1/2 t. baking powder
1 c. butter, softened
8-oz. pkg. cream cheese, softened
1 T. milk

1 T. sugar
1 egg yolk, beaten
12-oz. can fruit or poppy seed filling
Garnish: powdered sugar

Combine flour and baking powder in a small bowl; set aside. Blend butter, cream cheese, milk and sugar; add egg yolk, then flour mixture. Form dough into a ball; wrap in wax paper and chill for several hours or overnight. Roll out 1/4-inch thick on a floured surface; cut out with a 2-inch round cookie cutter. Arrange 3 inches apart on ungreased baking sheets. Make a thumbprint impression in center of each round; fill with one teaspoon filling. Bake at 400 degrees for 10 minutes or until golden. Remove to a platter; let cool and sprinkle with powdered sugar. Makes about 4 dozen.

When cookie baking is
a family affair,
dress little ones in
washable clothes and aprons.
Be sure to take lots of pictures!

Frost-Kissed CUT-OUTS

Lemon Zest Cookies

Weda Mosellie
Phillipsburg, NJ

Pastries are a big part of our Italian family's Christmas tradition, including these cookies.

3 c. all-purpose flour
4 eggs, beaten
8-oz. pkg. cream cheese,
   softened
1 c. sugar

1/4 c. oil
juice and zest of 2 lemons
1/2 t. baking powder
1/2 t. baking soda

Combine all ingredients in a large mixing bowl; mix well to form a dough. Roll out to 1/2-inch thickness and chill for one hour. Cut into circles using a glass or round cookie cutter. Arrange on a greased baking sheet and bake at 350 degrees for 13 to 15 minutes; let cool. Dip tops of cookies into glaze; let dry. Makes 2 to 2-1/2 dozen.

Glaze:

1 c. powdered sugar
zest of 1 lemon

juice of 1 to 2 lemons

Combine powdered sugar and zest. Add enough lemon juice to make a thin consistency, mixing well.

Mmm, instead of frosting the tops of cut-out cookies, frost the bottoms of two cookies and gently press together to make a sweetly simple cookie sandwich.

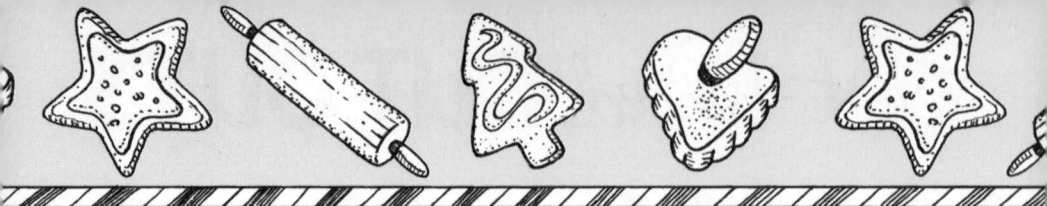

Pepparkakor

Virginia Watson
Scranton, PA

This is a Swedish cookie commonly made for St. Lucia's Day.

1-1/2 c. butter, softened
2-1/4 c. sugar, divided
2 eggs, beaten
1/2 c. molasses
4 c. all-purpose flour

1 T. ground ginger
1-1/2 t. cinnamon
1-1/2 t. ground cloves
2 t. baking soda
1/2 t. salt

Blend together butter and 2 cups sugar in a medium bowl; add eggs and molasses, mixing well. Stir in remaining ingredients to make a stiff dough, adding more flour if necessary. Roll out on a floured surface to 1/8 to 1/4-inch thickness. Cut with cookie cutters and sprinkle with remaining sugar. Arrange on greased baking sheets; bake at 350 degrees for 5 to 6 minutes or until lightly golden. Makes 5 to 6 dozen.

Metal-rimmed key tags make gift tags a snap. Simply replace the string with a glittery silver pipe cleaner, tie on and you're done!

Frost-Kissed **CUT-OUTS**

Gingerbread Cookies

Peggy Remizowski
New York Mills, NY

This recipe can be used to make gingerbread houses too!

1 c. shortening
1 c. sugar
1 egg, beaten
1 c. molasses
2 T. white vinegar
5 c. all-purpose flour

1 T. ground ginger
1-1/2 t. baking soda
1 t. cinnamon
1 t. ground cloves
1/2 t. salt

Blend together shortening and sugar; beat in egg, molasses and vinegar. Sift dry ingredients together; blend into shortening mixture. Chill for at least 3 hours. Roll out 1/4-inch thick on a lightly floured surface. Cut into shapes with cookie cutters; arrange on greased baking sheets. Bake at 350 degrees for 8 minutes. Cool slightly on sheets; remove to wire racks and cool completely. Decorate with frosting. Makes 5 dozen.

Frosting:

4-1/2 c. powdered sugar
6 T. butter, melted
6 T. milk
2 T. vanilla extract

1 T. lemon juice
Optional: few drops food
   coloring

Combine all ingredients in a medium bowl. Beat with an electric mixer on low speed until smooth.

Use a prancing reindeer cookie cutter for Gingerbread Cookies... they'll look sweet-as-can-be dancing around the edges of a favorite plate.

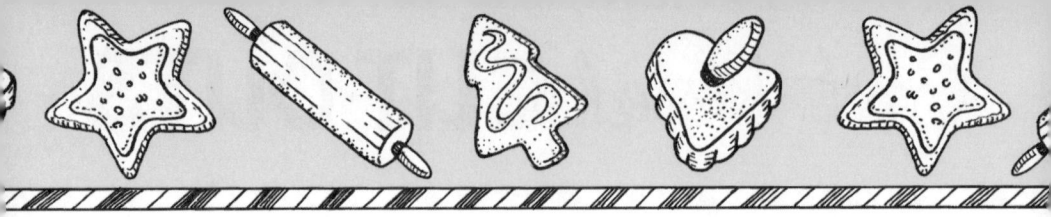

Jean's Sugar Cookies

Glenna Carroll
Golden, OK

This recipe has been in my family for over 40 years. I remember the first time my mother made it when I was 10 years old. Over the years, my children's teachers have requested it for school parties, I've made it for my son's office, and I even sell it in our country store on special occasions. What great memories I have from these wonderful cookies!

1/2 c. shortening	3-1/2 c. all-purpose flour
1/2 c. butter, softened	2 t. baking powder
1 c. sugar	1-1/2 t. vanilla extract
3 eggs, beaten	

Blend together shortening and butter, gradually adding sugar. Add eggs; beat well. Blend in remaining ingredients until smooth. Chill for at least 3 hours or overnight. Divide dough in half. Roll out one half on a lightly floured surface to 1/4-inch thickness, chilling remaining half until ready to use. Cut into shapes with floured cookie cutters; arrange cookies on ungreased baking sheets. Bake at 350 degrees for 10 to 12 minutes until edges are golden. Cool completely on wire racks before frosting. Makes 4 to 5 dozen.

Frosting:

3 T. butter, softened	2-1/2 to 3 T. evaporated milk
2-1/2 to 3 c. powdered sugar	1 t. vanilla extract

Cream butter; beat in sugar alternately with milk and vanilla, adding more sugar or milk as needed to make frosting spreadable.

Frost-Kissed CUT-OUTS

Buttermilk Sugar Cookies

Meri Hebert
Cheboygan, MI

*I make these for every holiday...it's the softest cookie ever,
and everyone always wants the recipe.*

2 c. sugar
2 c. shortening
4 eggs
1 T. vanilla extract
2 c. buttermilk
6 c. all-purpose flour

1 T. plus 1 t. baking powder
2 t. baking soda
1/2 t. salt
Garnish: 16-oz. container
   favorite frosting
Optional: candy sprinkles

Blend together sugar, shortening and eggs; add vanilla and buttermilk
and set aside. Combine flour, baking powder, baking soda and salt;
stir into sugar mixture. Add more flour as needed to make a firm
dough. Chill for 2 to 3 hours or overnight. Roll out 1/4-inch thick on
a floured surface; cut out with cookie cutters. Bake on greased baking
sheets at 350 degrees for 7 to 8 minutes. Let cool; frost and decorate
as desired. Makes about 6 dozen.

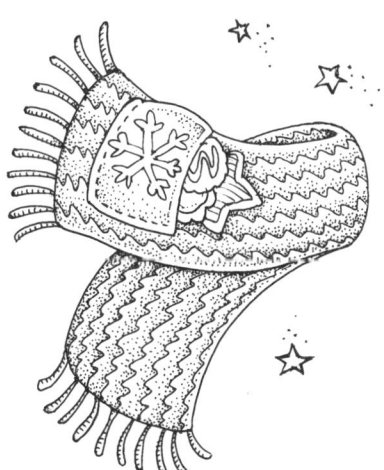

*All bundled up!
Stitch a square fleece
pocket to a warm & fuzzy
scarf and tuck plastic-
wrapped cut-out cookies
into the pocket...a gift that's
sure to please.*

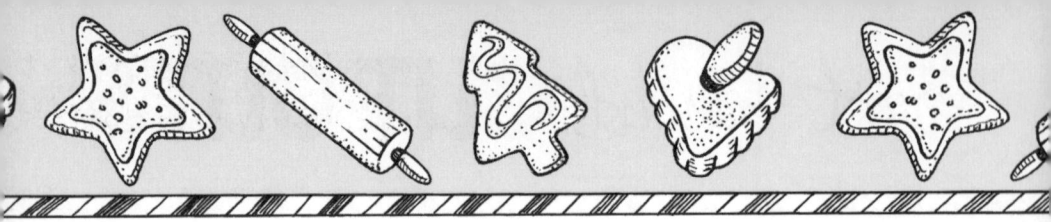

Baby Cakes

Renée Spec
Crescent, PA

*These are delicate cookies to make with your smallest cookie cutters.
I use a tiny flower-shaped cutter.*

1 c. butter, softened
2 c. all-purpose flour

1/3 c. whipping cream
Garnish: sugar

Combine butter, flour and cream; mix well and chill. Roll out 1/8 to
1/4-inch thick on a lightly floured surface. Cut with tiny cookie cutters;
place close together on ungreased baking sheets. Pierce each cookie
several times with a fork; sprinkle lightly with sugar. Bake at
375 degrees for about 8 minutes, until lightly golden. Assemble
cookies in pairs with Creamy Filling. Makes 4-1/2 dozen.

Creamy Filling:

1/4 c. butter, softened
3/4 c. powdered sugar

1 t. vanilla extract

Mix ingredients together until smooth.

Frost-Kissed CUT-OUTS

Crisp Sugar Cookies

*Marie Martin
Vestal, NY*

*For a fun afternoon, get the kids or friends involved in whipping up
this easy cookie recipe...don't forget to take lots of pictures!*

2/3 c. butter, softened
3/4 c. sugar
1 t. vanilla extract
1 egg
1 T. plus 1 t. milk
2 c. all-purpose flour

1-1/2 t. baking powder
1/2 t. nutmeg
1/4 t. salt
Garnish: assorted coarse
   decorator sugars

Blend butter, sugar and vanilla. Add egg; beat until light and fluffy.
Stir in milk; set aside. Sift together remaining ingredients except
garnish and add to butter mixture; mix well. Chill for one hour. Roll
out dough 1/8-inch thick on a floured surface; cut with cookie cutters
as desired. Place on greased baking sheets; sprinkle with coarse sugar.
Bake at 350 degrees for 6 to 8 minutes, until edges are golden. Let
cool before removing from baking sheets. Makes 2 dozen.

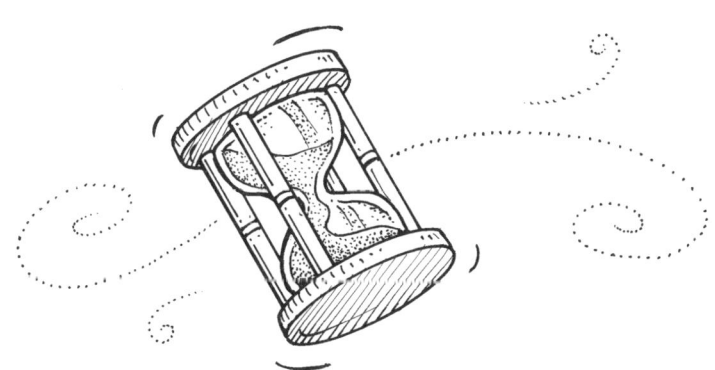

Kids have a hard time waiting for cookie dough to chill.
Help pass the time by playing silly games like
"I Spy" or "Rock, Paper, Scissors."

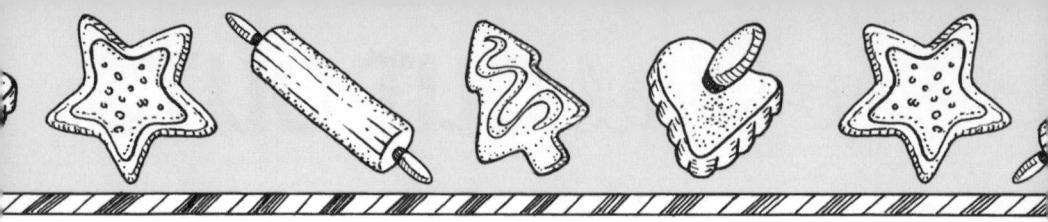

Pepper Cookies

Lisa Ashton
Aston, PA

This spicy little cookie goes great with all the other holiday treats!

1/2 c. butter
1/2 c. sugar
1/2 c. dark corn syrup
1-1/2 t. vinegar
1 egg, beaten
2-1/4 c. all-purpose flour

1/2 t. baking soda
1/2 t. ground ginger
1/2 t. cinnamon
1/2 t. ground cloves
1/4 t. pepper

Melt butter in a medium saucepan; add sugar, corn syrup and vinegar and bring just to a boil. Remove from heat immediately; let cool to room temperature. Stir in egg and set aside. Combine flour, baking soda and spices in a bowl; add to egg mixture, mixing well. Cover and chill for 3 hours to overnight. Divide dough into 4 portions, continuing to chill each portion until ready to roll out. Roll dough onto a lightly floured surface to 1/8-inch thickness. Cut into shapes with cookie cutters and arrange on greased baking sheets. Bake at 375 degrees for 4 to 5 minutes or until golden around the edges. Immediately transfer cookies to cooling rack. Makes 10 dozen.

Use a smaller cookie cutter to create a cut-out inside a cookie. Fill the cut-out with crushed hard candy before baking. As it bakes and melts, the candy magically creates a stained-glass look.

Frost-Kissed CUT-OUTS

Old-Fashioned Tea Cake Cookies

Wendy Windal
Burkburnett, TX

These will disappear as fast as you can make them!

1 c. shortening
1-1/2 c. sugar
3 eggs
1 t. baking soda
1/2 c. buttermilk
5 c. all-purpose flour
2 t. baking powder
2 t. vanilla extract

Mix shortening, sugar and eggs together; set aside. Dissolve baking soda in buttermilk; stir in flour, baking powder and vanilla. Beat into shortening mixture; roll out on a floured surface to 1/4-inch thickness. Cut with a round cookie cutter; place on ungreased baking sheets. Bake at 400 degrees for 10 to 15 minutes or until golden. Makes 6 to 7 dozen.

Jam Tea

Kristin Blanton
Big Bear City, CA

Try using your favorite flavor of jam...I like this tea with strawberry, apricot or even mint.

4 to 6 t. raspberry jam, divided
1 teapot brewed English
   breakfast tea
sugar to taste
Optional: whipped cream

Place one teaspoon jam in bottom of each teacup; pour hot tea over jam and stir. Add sugar to taste and top with whipped cream, if desired. Makes 4 to 6 cups of tea.

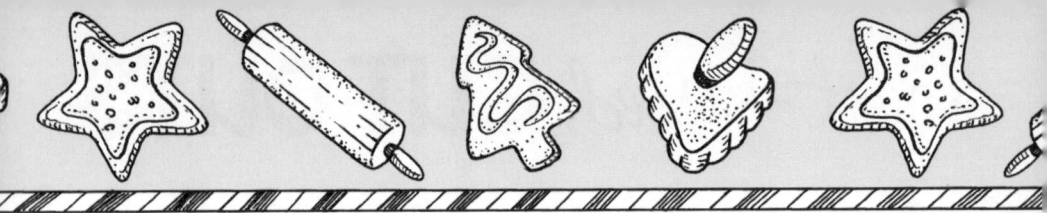

Laurie's Special Sugar Cookies

Laurie Costa
Maxwell, CA

*My love of baking came from making delicious cookie creations with
my grandma…learning how to measure, how to blend ingredients,
and practicing my patience as I waited for the cookies to bake.
Now that I have 2 daughters of my own, baking (and eating!) cookies
has become our family tradition, especially at Christmas.*

2 c. all-purpose flour	3/4 c. sugar
1-1/2 t. baking powder	1 egg, beaten
1/4 t. salt	1 T. milk
1/4 c. plus 2 T. margarine	1 t. vanilla extract
1/3 c. shortening	Optional: cream cheese frosting

Combine flour, baking powder and salt; set aside. Beat margarine
and shortening with an electric mixer until soft; add sugar and
beat until fluffy. Add egg, milk and vanilla; beat well. Gradually
add flour mixture and mix until blended. Cover and chill for 2 hours.
Roll dough out 1/8-inch thick on a lightly floured surface. Cut with
floured cookie cutters; arrange cookies on greased baking sheets.
Bake at 375 degrees for 7 to 8 minutes until just golden around
the edges. Cool completely on a wire rack and frost as desired.
Makes 1-1/2 to 2 dozen.

For a sweet cookie topping without using frosting, simply dust powdered sugar or baking cocoa over warm cookies.

Frost-Kissed **CUT-OUTS**

Old-Fashioned Gingerbread Boys

*Christine Waterbury
Sheboygan, WI*

This is my Grandma Rena's recipe. My fondest memories are of her baking these cookies every Christmas...she always baked so much love into them.

1/3 c. shortening	1 t. salt
1 c. brown sugar, packed	1 t. allspice
1-1/2 c. dark molasses	1 t. ground ginger
2/3 c. cold water	1 t. ground cloves
7 c. all-purpose flour	1 t. cinnamon
2 t. baking soda	

Combine shortening, brown sugar and molasses; mix well. Stir in water; set aside. Sift together flour and remaining ingredients in a large bowl; add to molasses mixture and mix thoroughly. Divide dough into 4 portions: chill for 3 to 4 hours. Roll out one portion at a time, keeping remaining dough cool until ready to use. Roll to 1/2-inch thickness; cut with medium-sized, floured gingerbread boy cookie cutters. Arrange on greased baking sheets; bake at 375 degrees for 10 to 12 minutes. Cool completely on wire racks and frost as desired. Store in airtight containers. Makes about 7 dozen.

Dip cooled cookies halfway into warm, melted chocolate for a yummy treat. Set on wax paper to let chocolate cool and harden.

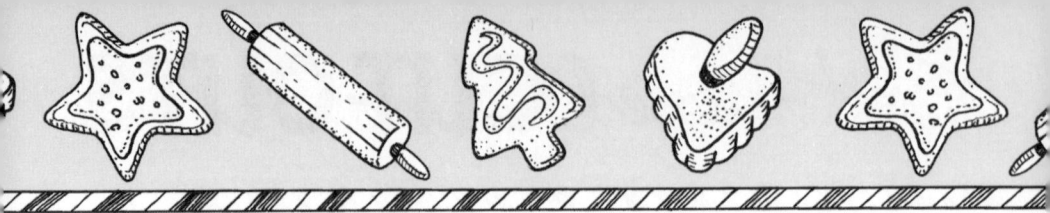

Christmas Cookies

Flo Burtnett
Gage, OK

Get creative...try making pretty poinsettia leaves on these cookies!

1/2 c. margarine, softened
1/2 c. cream cheese, softened
1-1/4 c. powdered sugar
1 egg
1-1/2 t. vanilla extract

1/4 t. salt
1/4 t. baking powder
3 c. all-purpose flour

Beat margarine, cream cheese and sugar until fluffy; add egg, vanilla, salt and baking powder. Mix in flour until dough holds together; form into a ball. Wrap in plastic wrap; chill for at least one hour. Roll dough out on a floured surface to 1/4-inch thickness; cut with round cookie cutters. Bake at 350 degrees for 15 minutes or until golden; cool. Frost and decorate as desired. Makes 4 to 5 dozen.

Frosting:

2 c. powdered sugar
1/2 t. vanilla extract
2 to 3 T. milk

Garnish: green and red
tube frosting

Combine sugar and vanilla in a small mixing bowl; add enough milk to make a glaze consistency. Mix well; spread on each cookie and let dry. Garnish with red flowers and green leaves on each cookie using tube frosting.

Look for clever containers to tote cookie swap goodies...a vintage milk bottle carrier is ideal.

Frost-Kissed CUT-OUTS

Good Roll-Out Cookies

Debi DeVore
Dover, OH

This recipe makes enough for a cookie swap with plenty left over for friends, neighbors and Santa!

1 T. plus 1 t. baking soda	8 eggs, beaten
2 c. sour cream	2 t. vanilla extract
4 c. butter, softened	4 t. baking powder
4 c. sugar	12 c. all-purpose flour

Dissolve baking soda in sour cream; add butter and sugar. Mix well; stir in eggs and vanilla. Mix in baking powder and flour; roll dough out to 1/4-inch thickness. Cut out with cookie cutters; place on greased and floured baking sheets. Bake at 325 degrees for 8 to 10 minutes; cool. Spread frosting over the top. Makes 12 to 14 dozen.

Frosting:

2-lb. pkg. powdered sugar	8-oz. pkg. cream cheese,
2 c. butter, softened	softened
2 to 4 t. vanilla extract	1/4 to 1/2 c. milk

Mix sugar, butter, vanilla and cream cheese together; add enough milk to make desired thickness.

For an extra-special touch, pipe frosting onto cookies in a snowflake, star or tree shape, then dust with sanding sugar...so glittery!

You're invited to a

COOKIE EXCHANGE!

WHEN: _____

HOSTED
  BY: _____

WHERE: _____

_____

_____

R.S.V.P. _____

Please bring: _____

Use our invitation to send to family & friends!
Just copy, cut out & color with markers,
colored pencils or glitter pens. oh so easy!

Razzle-Dazzle
DROP COOKIES

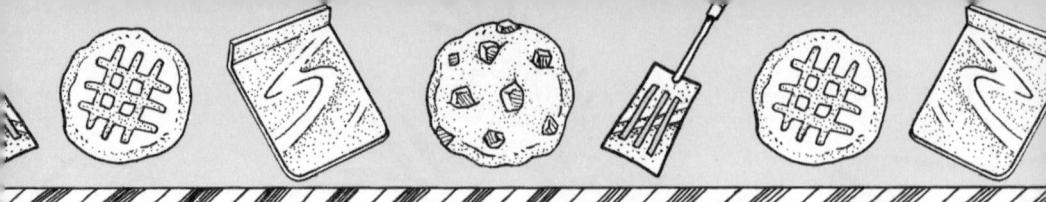

Chewy Molasses Dreams

Lisa Case
Fresno, CA

You'll love eating this spicy, sweet cookie...better than store-bought!

3/4 c. shortening
1-1/2 c. sugar, divided
1 egg
1/3 c. molasses
2-1/3 c. all-purpose flour
2 t. baking soda

2 t. ground ginger
2 t. cinnamon
2 t. nutmeg
1 t. ground cloves
1/4 t. salt

Combine shortening, one cup sugar, egg and molasses; mix well. Blend in flour, baking soda, spices and salt. Shape into one-inch balls; roll in remaining sugar. Arrange on ungreased baking sheets; flatten slightly. Bake at 350 degrees for 7 to 8 minutes. Makes 3 to 4 dozen.

Visit flea markets and gather up vintage colanders, flour sifters, teapots and teacups...terrific for tucking cookies into. Don't forget to tie on a recipe card too!

Razzle-Dazzle DROP COOKIES

Chow Mein Cookies

Mary Freireich
Dublin, OH

Here's a tasty butterscotch cookie with a twist...chow mein noodles!

2 6-oz. pkgs. semi-sweet
   chocolate chips
2 6-oz. pkgs. butterscotch chips
2 3-oz. cans chow mein noodles
1/2 c. cashew pieces

Melt together chocolate and butterscotch chips over low heat in a saucepan; blend well. Stir in chow mein noodles and cashews. Drop by teaspoonfuls onto wax paper-lined baking sheets. Let set until firm. Makes 2 to 3 dozen.

Eggnog

Janet Pritchard
Killeen, TX

It just wouldn't be Christmas without eggnog!

2 c. whipping cream
1/3 c. powdered sugar
1 t. rum extract
1/2 t. nutmeg
1/4 t. allspice
1 qt. vanilla ice cream, softened
4 qts. eggnog, divided
Garnish: cinnamon sticks, if
   desired

Whip cream with powdered sugar, rum extract, nutmeg and allspice until stiff peaks form; set aside. Combine ice cream and 2 cups eggnog in a blender; blend until just smooth. Pour into a large punch bowl; stir in remaining eggnog. Fold in whipped cream mixture just until fluffy. Makes about 5 quarts.

Cookie cutters make whimsical gift bag tie-ons...
a heart or bunny for springtime, flag for summer,
oak leaf or acorn in the fall and a plump snowman
or snowflake in the winter.

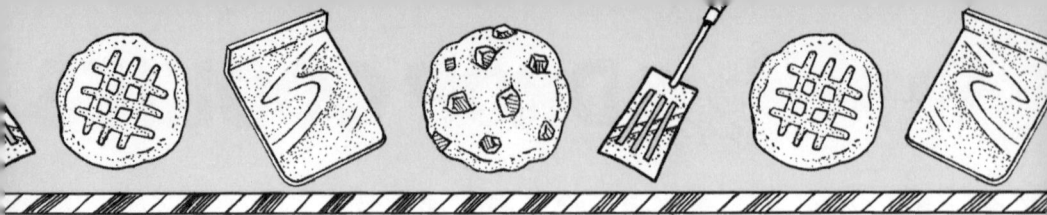

Meringue Kisses

Candy Hannigan
Monument, CO

Try piping these out in different holiday shapes...snowmen are cute with chocolate chips for eyes and buttons, and a cherry for its nose!

3 egg whites
1/4 t. cream of tartar
2/3 c. sugar
1/2 c. mini semi-sweet
    chocolate chips

1/2 t. peppermint extract
several drops red or green
    food coloring

Beat egg whites with an electric mixer on high speed until foamy; beat in cream of tartar. Slowly beat in sugar one tablespoon at a time until dissolved and stiff peaks form. Fold in chocolate chips, extract and food coloring. Drop mixture by teaspoonfuls onto parchment paper-lined baking sheets. Bake at 275 degrees for 30 minutes; turn off oven and leave overnight. Store in an airtight container at room temperature. Makes 2 to 3 dozen.

Fold glittery paper into a cone shape and secure the edges with tape. Fill with a variety of cookies... what a great party favor!

Mint Petites

Debbie Pecore
Charlton, MA

If you're a fan of mint-chocolate, try these!

1/4 c. sugar
1 c. margarine, softened
1/4 to 1/2 t. peppermint extract
1/2 t. vanilla extract

2 c. all-purpose flour
Garnish: vanilla or chocolate
frosting, peppermint or
chocolate mint candies

In a large bowl, blend sugar and margarine together until fluffy. Add extracts; mix well. Stir in flour and blend well. Shape into one-inch balls; place on ungreased baking sheets and flatten slightly. Bake at 375 degrees for 12 minutes or until lightly golden. Let cool. Frost with vanillia frosting and sprinkle with crushed peppermint candies, or with chocolate frosting and top with chocolate mints cut into triangles. Makes 2 to 3 dozen.

White Hot Chocolate

Dawn Brown
Vandenberg AFB, CA

This hot chocolate will warm you head-to-toe.

12-oz. bar white chocolate,
   finely chopped
6 c. milk
2 c. heavy cream

1 t. vanilla extract
Garnish: whipped cream,
   cinnamon, milk chocolate
   shavings, candy canes

Place white chocolate in a medium bowl; set aside. Combine milk and cream in a saucepan; heat over medium heat until bubbles begin to form around edges, about 4 minutes. Do not boil. Pour over white chocolate. When chocolate begins to melt, gently stir to combine. Whisk in vanilla. Top with whipped cream, cinnamon or chocolate shavings. Add a candy cane too! Serve immediately. Makes 8 cups.

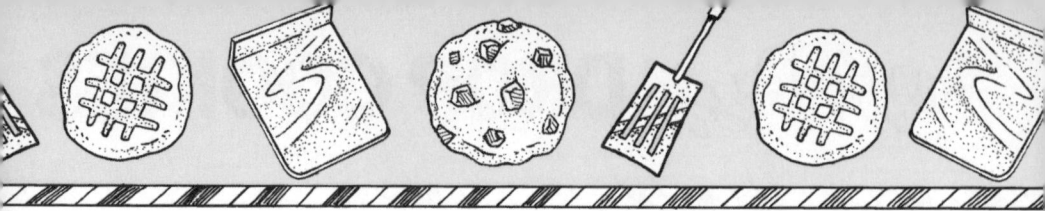

Grandma's Ginger Cookies

Andrea Barclay
Somerset, PA

My Grandma Kintigh used to make these all the time and I ate them with butter on top. I make them now for my friends & family and my kids love them, although they don't use the butter...they just want to eat them!

3/4 c. shortening
1 c. dark brown sugar, packed
1/2 c. dark molasses
1 egg
2 c. all-purpose flour
1/2 t. salt

2 t. baking soda
1 t. cinnamon
1 t. ground ginger
1/8 t. ground cloves
Garnish: sugar

Blend together shortening, sugar, molasses and egg; set aside. Mix together flour, salt, baking soda and spices; add slowly to shortening mixture. Mix well. Place sugar in a small bowl; drop dough by teaspoonfuls into sugar. Roll into balls; arrange on ungreased baking sheets. Bake at 350 degrees for 8 to 10 minutes, until just set and starting to crack. Let stand on baking sheets for one to 2 minutes; remove to cooling racks. Store in an airtight container. Makes 4 to 5 dozen.

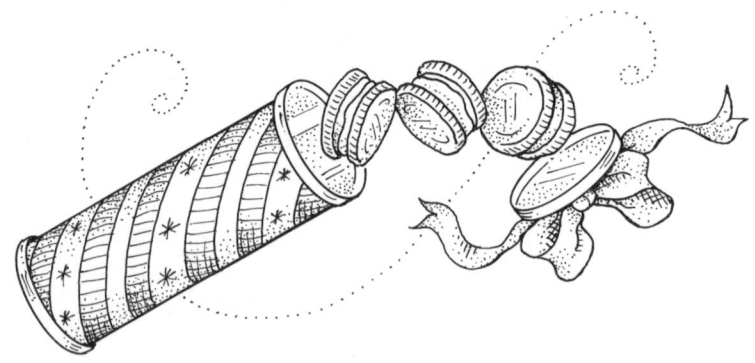

Stack cookies inside an empty oatmeal or potato chip canister that's been covered in pretty paper...just top with a bow!

Razzle-Dazzle DROP COOKIES

Holiday Gumdrop Cookies

Pat Habiger
Spearville, KS

*Christmas just wouldn't be the same without
Holiday Gumdrop Cookies!*

1/2 c. butter, softened
1/2 c. margarine, softened
1 c. sugar
2 eggs
1 t. vanilla extract
2 c. all-purpose flour
1 t. baking powder

1/2 t. baking soda
1/4 t. salt
2 c. quick-cooking oatmeal,
   uncooked
1 c. flaked coconut
1 c. pecans, coarsely chopped
1 c. gumdrops, sliced

Blend together butter, margarine and sugar. Stir in eggs, one at a time, and vanilla until well mixed; set aside. Sift together flour, baking powder, baking soda and salt; add to butter mixture and mix well. Stir in remaining ingredients just until mixed; refrigerate dough several hours or overnight. With floured hands, roll dough into 1-1/2 inch balls. Bake on parchment paper-lined baking sheets for 10 to 15 minutes at 375 degrees. Makes 2 to 3 dozen.

Want ready-made cookies at your fingertips? Just freeze them! Most cookie doughs freeze well and will stay fresh for 4 to 6 weeks and baked cookies for 3 to 4 weeks. When it's cookie baking time, just let them come to room temperature and bake according to the recipe.

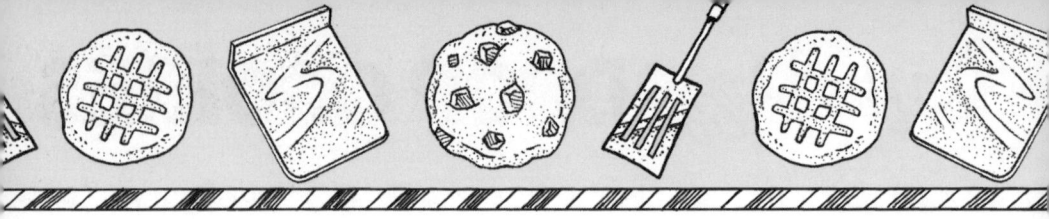

Brown Sugar Drops

Andrea Barclay
Somerset, PA

*My husband's grandmother gave this recipe to me shortly after
we were married. She doesn't bake anymore, so now it's nice
that we can make these cookies for her.*

1 egg, beaten
1 c. brown sugar, packed
1 t. vanilla extract
1/2 c. all-purpose flour

1/4 t. baking soda
1/4 t. salt
1-1/2 c. chopped walnuts

Stir together egg, brown sugar and vanilla. Stir in flour, baking soda
and salt; add walnuts. Drop by teaspoonfuls onto well-greased, floured
baking sheets. Bake at 350 degrees for 7 to 9 minutes or until cookies
start to turn golden at edges. Remove from baking sheets immediately.
Makes about 4 dozen.

Mexican Hot Chocolate

Jen Licon-Conner
Gooseberry Patch

This is serious hot chocolate...almost a dessert in itself!

3.3-oz. tablet Mexican
   chocolate, diced

1-1/4 c. milk
1-1/4 c. half-and-half

Combine all ingredients in a saucepan;
bring to a simmer, stirring until chocolate
is melted and well combined. Stir with a
whisk until fluffy before serving.
Makes 2-1/2 cups.

Razzle-Dazzle **DROP COOKIES**

Pecan Crispies

Emily Robinette
Xenia, OH

Grandma Alice made these every Christmas and topped them with red and green sugar. For me, making them pretty took a little more practice. Don't worry if they don't look perfect...they sure will taste perfect!

1/2 c. shortening
1/2 c. margarine, softened
2-1/2 c. brown sugar, packed
2 eggs, beaten
2-1/2 c. all-purpose flour

1/2 t. baking soda
1/4 t. salt
1 c. chopped pecans
Garnish: sugar

Combine shortening, margarine and brown sugar; mix well. Beat in eggs; set aside. Sift together flour, baking soda and salt; add to shortening mixture and mix well. Stir in pecans. Drop by heaping teaspoonfuls about 3 inches apart onto greased baking sheets. Press down using a greased, sugared glass; sprinkle tops with sugar. Bake at 350 degrees for 12 to 15 minutes; cookies will be dark when done. Makes 3 to 4 dozen.

To minimize spreading in drop cookies, let the baking sheets cool between batches and only grease them if the recipe calls for it.

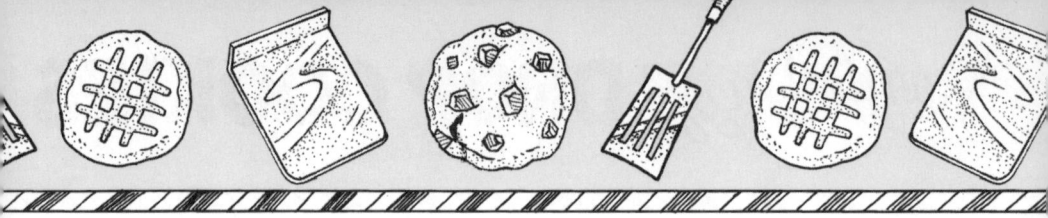

Health Nut Cookies

Cyndi Little
Whitsett, NC

This recipe came from a good friend in our community...she entered it in a baking contest in the 50's and won a brand-new range presented to her by Ronald Reagan! She thought it was so special, she never took the plastic off!

1 c. butter
1 c. brown sugar, packed
1 c. sugar
2 eggs
1 t. vanilla extract
2 c. all-purpose flour
1-1/2 c. quick-cooking oats, uncooked

1-1/2 t. baking powder
1/2 t. salt
1 c. chopped dates
1 c. raisins
1 c. flaked coconut
1 c. chopped pecans
Optional: pecan halves

Blend together butter, sugars, eggs and vanilla; add flour, oats, baking powder and salt. Mix well. Stir in dates, raisins, coconut and pecans. Drop by teaspoonfuls onto greased baking sheets; flatten slightly. Top each cookie with a pecan half, if desired. Bake at 325 degrees for 15 minutes. Remove from baking sheets while still warm. Makes about 6 dozen.

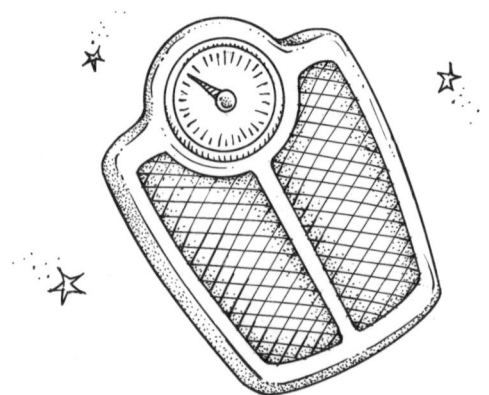

A balanced diet is a cookie in each hand.
-Unknown

Almond-Pine Nut Cookies

Annette Lacombe
Norwich, CT

The taste of almonds and the crunchiness of pine nuts.

7-oz. pkg. almond paste, diced
1/3 c. sugar
2 egg whites, divided

1/2 t. vanilla extract
3 T. all-purpose flour
1/2 c. pine nuts

Beat together almond paste, sugar and one egg white until smooth. Blend in remaining egg white, then vanilla. Stir until flour until dough forms. Drop by heaping teaspoonfuls, 2 inches apart, onto parchment paper-lined baking sheets. Press 1/2 teaspoon pine nuts onto each cookie. Position oven rack in top third of oven; bake at 325 degrees until edges are golden, about 15 minutes. Let cool on wire rack. Makes about 2 dozen.

For an extra touch, roll chilled dough in colored or cinnamon sugar, chopped nuts or flaked coconut.

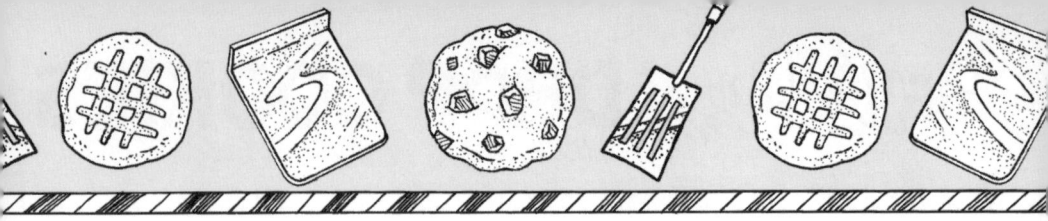

Kris Kringles

Eleanor Bartz
Shelby, IN

The jolly old elf himself can't resist these!

1/2 c. butter, softened
1/4 c. sugar
1 egg, separated
1 T. orange zest
1 t. lemon zest

1 t. lemon juice
1 c. cake flour
1/8 t. salt
1/2 c. finely chopped nuts
9 maraschino cherries, halved

Thoroughly blend butter and sugar. Beat egg yolk; add to butter mixture along with zests and lemon juice. Mix well. Stir in flour and salt. Chill until firm. Form 1/2-inch balls; dip in beaten egg white and roll lightly in nuts. Place on greased baking sheets; press a cherry half in center of each. Bake at 325 degrees for 20 minutes. Makes 1-1/2 dozen.

Parchment paper is terrific for shaping into cones to hold icings for piping. And it's easy to find in rolls, circles or sheets at craft stores or supermarkets with cake-decorating supplies.

Christmas Crinkle Cookies

Rachael Hall
McDonald, PA

Chocolatey morsels with a snowy coating of powdered sugar...yummy!

12-oz. pkg. semi-sweet chocolate chips, divided	1 c. sugar
1-1/2 c. all-purpose flour	6 T. butter, softened
1-1/2 t. baking powder	1-1/2 t. vanilla extract
1/4 t. salt	2 eggs
	3/4 c. powdered sugar

Place one cup chocolate chips in a microwave-safe bowl. Microwave on high setting for one minute; stir. Microwave at additional 10-second intervals, stirring until smooth. Cool to room temperature. Combine flour, baking powder and salt in a small bowl; set aside. Blend sugar, butter and vanilla in a large bowl; beat in melted chocolate. Add eggs one at a time, stirring well after each. Gradually beat in flour mixture; stir in remaining chips. Chill just until firm. Shape into 1-1/2 inch balls; roll generously in powdered sugar. Place on ungreased baking sheets. Bake at 350 degrees for 10 to 15 minutes, until sides are set and centers are still slightly soft. Cool on baking sheets 2 minutes; place on wire racks to cool completely. Makes 4 to 5 dozen.

Make cookie gifts festive and fun! Stack cookies inside vintage glassware or fill a retro recipe box or old-fashioned ice cream mold. Even the simplest cardboard box or paper bag can be transformed tied up with ribbon and greenery.

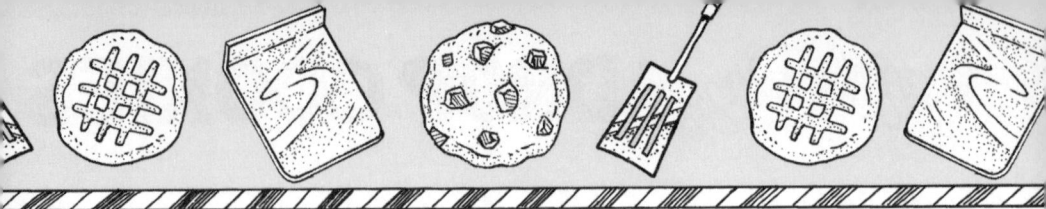

Heavenly Cookies

Joy Diomede
Double Oak, TX

Craving chocolate? Try these double-chocolate and candy bar cookies!

1 c. butter, softened
2-1/2 c. powdered sugar
2 eggs
2 t. vanilla extract
2-1/2 c. all-purpose flour
1 t. baking soda
1 t. salt

1/2 c. white chocolate chips
1-1/2 c. semi-sweet chocolate chunks
4 1.4-oz. toffee candy bars, crushed
Optional: 1/2 c. chopped pecans

Combine butter, sugar, eggs and vanilla; mix well. Add flour, baking soda and salt; mix until well blended. Stir in chocolate chips, chocolate chunks, candy bar pieces and nuts, if using. Drop by tablespoonfuls onto ungreased baking sheets. Bake at 350 degrees for 12 to 15 minutes, or until golden. Makes 2 dozen.

Shipping cookies is a snap...just follow these pointers. Choose firm cookies such as sliced, drop or bar cookies; avoid frosted or filled ones. Line a sturdy box with plastic bubble wrap and pack cookies in a single layer with wax paper between the layers.

Chocolate Snowballs

Arlene Grimm
Decatur, AL

Rolling cooled cookies in powdered sugar makes these buttery cookies even richer.

2 c. sugar
1/2 c. milk
3/4 c. margarine
6 T. baking cocoa
3 c. quick-cooking oats,
    uncooked

1 c. chopped pecans
1 t. vanilla extract
Garnish: powdered sugar

Combine sugar, milk, margarine and cocoa in a saucepan. Bring to a boil over medium heat, stirring constantly. When mixture comes to a boil, remove from heat; stir in oats, pecans and vanilla. Allow to cool to room temperature. Shape into one-inch balls; roll in powdered sugar. Keep refrigerated in an airtight container. Makes about 3 dozen.

For a whimsical gift, line a vintage pail with a kitchen towel and tuck freshly baked cookies inside.

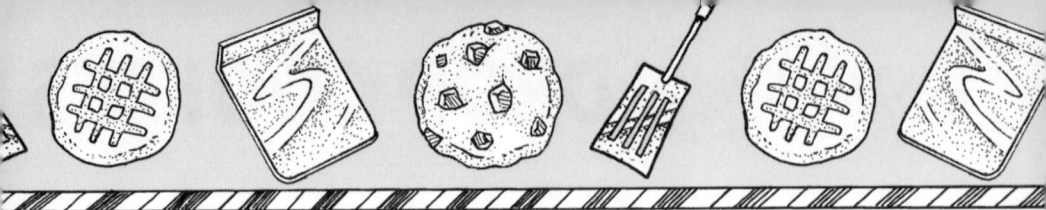

Whoopie Pies

Brenda Doak
Delaware, OH

Not pies at all, but soft, chocolatey cookies!

2 c. sugar
1/2 c. shortening
2 eggs
1 t. vanilla extract
4 c. all-purpose flour
1/2 c. baking cocoa

2 t. baking soda
1/2 t. salt
1 c. milk
1 T. vinegar
1 c. warm water

Blend together sugar, shortening, eggs and vanilla; set aside. Sift together flour, cocoa, baking soda and salt; set aside. Combine milk and vinegar; stir to blend and set aside. Add flour mixture to sugar mixture alternately with milk mixture and warm water. Drop by heaping teaspoonfuls onto lightly greased baking sheets. Bake at 425 degrees for 7 to 10 minutes; let cool. Spread filling on the bottom of one cookie; top with another cookie to make a sandwich. Makes 3 dozen.

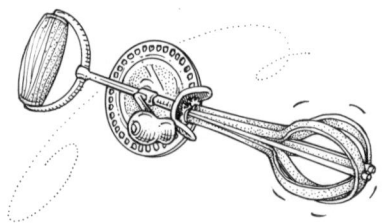

Filling:

1-1/2 c. milk
1/2 c. plus 1-1/2 t. all-purpose
    flour
1/2 c. butter, softened

3/4 c. shortening
1 t. salt
1 t. vanilla extract
2 c. powdered sugar

Combine milk and flour in a saucepan; heat and stir until thick. Refrigerate until chilled. In a mixing bowl, combine chilled milk mixture and remaining ingredients. Beat until fluffy.

Snow Drops

Kari Mott
Galloway, OH

These are so good with a glass of milk!

1/2 c. margarine, softened	1/2 t. baking soda
1 c. brown sugar, packed	1/2 t. cinnamon
1 egg	1 c. dates, finely chopped
1 T. water	1/2 c. pecans, finely chopped
1 t. vanilla extract	Garnish: powdered sugar
1-1/2 c. all-purpose flour	

Blend together margarine, brown sugar, egg, water and vanilla; set aside. Combine flour, baking soda and cinnamon; stir into margarine mixture. Mix in dates and pecans. Drop by tablespoonfuls onto greased baking sheets. Bake for 8 to 10 minutes at 375 degrees. Roll in powdered sugar while still warm. Makes 3 dozen.

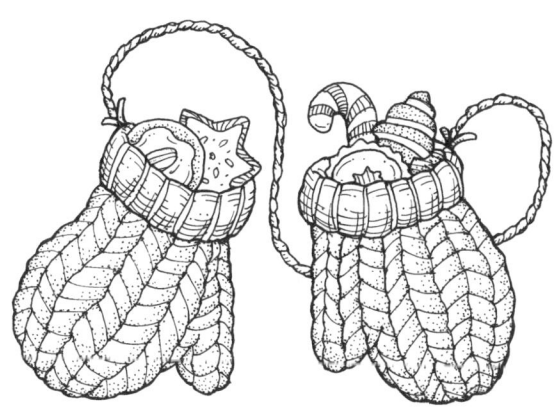

Let the season choose cookie packaging...cookies can be wrapped and tucked inside gardening gloves in summer or woolly mittens in winter. Add a homemade cocoa mix or fruity lemonade mix too!

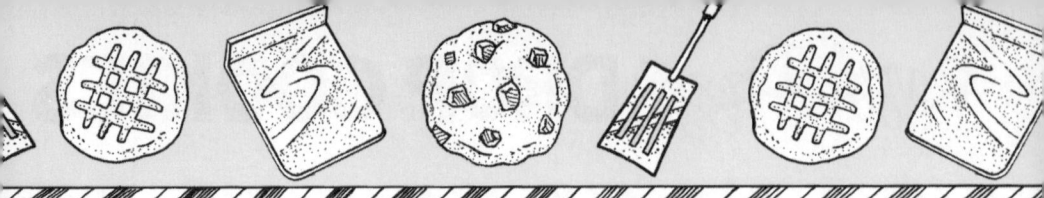

Grandma's Red-Hot Cookies

Susie Pechtl
Fargo, ND

When I was a child and went over to Grandma's house, I would always find these cookies in her kitchen cupboard.

1 c. sugar
1 c. powdered sugar
1 c. butter, softened
1 c. shortening
2 eggs
1/8 t. vanilla extract

4 c. all-purpose flour
2 t. cream of tartar
1 t. baking soda
Garnish: powdered sugar,
    red cinnamon candies

Combine all ingredients except garnish; mix well. Form into a roll; wrap in plastic wrap and chill thoroughly. Roll into one-inch balls; dip in powdered sugar. Flatten slightly with the bottom of a cup; top each with a cinnamon candy. Place on ungreased baking sheets. Bake at 350 degrees for about 9 minutes, watching carefully to avoid burning. Makes 6 dozen.

For a scrumptious change, substitute butterscotch, mint, cherry or cinnamon chips in place of the usual chocolate chips in favorite cookie recipes.

Razzle-Dazzle **DROP COOKIES**

Mom's Cream Cheese-Jelly Cookies

Dawn Menard
Seekonk, MA

A favorite my mother only made at Christmas time.

1 c. butter, softened
2 3-oz. pkgs. cream cheese,
   softened

2 c. all-purpose flour
Garnish: grape jelly

Blend together butter, cream cheese and flour in a large bowl to form dough. Refrigerate for one hour. Shape into one-inch balls; place on ungreased baking sheets. With your thumb, make an indentation on each ball. Bake at 325 degrees for 10 minutes, until golden. Let cool completely; place a spoonful of jelly in each indentation. Makes 2 to 3 dozen.

Holiday Pineapple Punch

Marci Grubb
Columbus, OH

For a festive touch, add a sprig of mint to your ice cube trays before freezing.

2 1-1/2 oz. pkgs. strawberry-
   flavored drink mix
2 c. sugar
4 qts. plus 3/4 c. water, divided
6-oz. can frozen pineapple
   juice concentrate

2-liter bottle lemon-lime soda
2-liter bottle strawberry soda
2-1/2 to 3 c. pineapple sherbet,
   softened

Combine drink mix, sugar and 4 quarts water in a large punch bowl; stir to dissolve. Add juice concentrate and remaining water, mix until concentrate is melted. Add sodas and sherbet; serve over ice. Makes about 2 gallons.

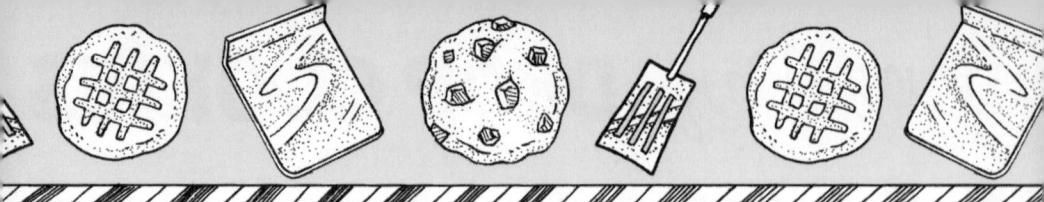

Peanut Butter Criss-Crosses

Jennifer Wiseman
Jamaica Plain, NY

Who doesn't love these traditional favorites? No cookie swap would be complete without them.

1 c. shortening
1 c. sugar
1 c. brown sugar, packed
2 eggs
1 t. vanilla extract

1 c. creamy peanut butter
3 c. all-purpose flour
1 t. baking soda
1 t. salt

Blend together shortening and sugars; mix in eggs and vanilla. Add peanut butter, mixing well. Set aside. Combine flour, baking soda and salt; slowly add to shortening mixture to make a stiff dough. Roll into one-inch balls; place on ungreased baking sheets. Flatten with a floured fork in a criss-cross pattern. Bake at 350 degrees for 9 to 11 minutes, until edges are golden. Makes 5 dozen.

Tie a pretty vintage silver fork on a jar filled with Peanut Butter Criss-Crosses. Just slip the recipe between the fork tines and friends will think of you each time they pull out the recipe!

Potato Chippers

Betty Kiphart
Muncie, IN

This recipe was given to me by a dear friend years ago. They've always been a favorite of mine (and everyone who samples them)!

1 c. shortening
1 c. sugar
1 c. brown sugar, packed
2 eggs
2 c. all-purpose flour

1 t. baking soda
1 t. salt
2 c. potato chips, crushed
1 c. chopped nuts

Blend shortening with sugars; add eggs and mix well. Sift together flour, baking soda and salt; add to shortening mixture. Stir in chips and nuts; shape into one-inch balls. Place on ungreased baking sheets; press down with a floured fork. Bake at 350 degrees for 10 to 12 minutes. Makes about 3 dozen.

A tier of cake plates is a fun way to serve cookies, candy or brownies on a buffet table.

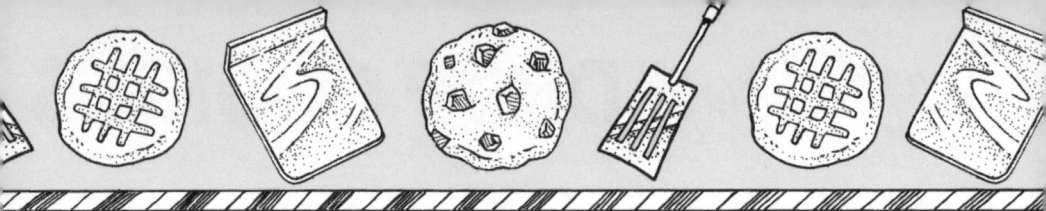

Moravian Spice Crisps

Mary Murray
Mount Vernon, OH

Similar versions of this spice cookie have been around since the 1700's. A crispy favorite...nice with a mug of warm cider.

3/4 c. all-purpose flour
1/2 t. baking powder
1/4 t. baking soda
1/4 t. salt
1/2 t. cinnamon
1/2 t. ground ginger

1/2 t. white pepper
1/4 t. ground cloves
1/3 c. light brown sugar, packed
3 T. butter, softened
1/4 c. light molasses

Combine flour, baking powder, baking soda, salt and spices; set aside. In a mixing bowl, blend brown sugar and butter with an electric mixer at low speed. Beat about 2 minutes on high speed until creamy. Beat in molasses at medium speed until blended. Using a spoon, stir in the flour mixture. Drop by rounded teaspoonfuls about 4 inches apart on greased baking sheets. Press each into a 2-inch circle. Bake at 350 degrees for 8 to 10 minutes. Let cool several minutes; remove to wire rack to cool completely. Store in tightly covered container. Makes about 3 dozen.

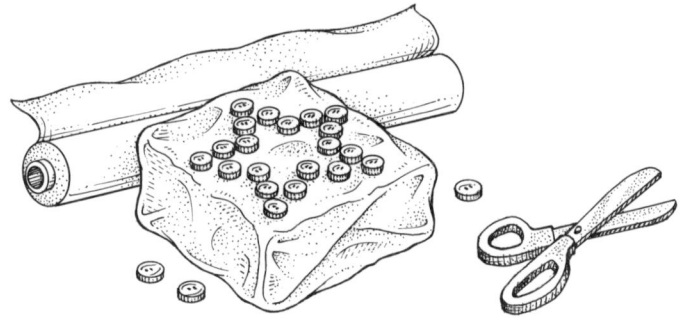

Once cookies are tucked inside a box for gift giving, wrap the box in kraft paper. On the box lid, arrange small ivory buttons in the shape of a star or wreath and glue in place. What a simple but sweet decoration.

One-Bowl Macaroons

Suzette Edwards
Glendale, AZ

If you love coconut, you'll love these too!

2 7-oz. pkgs. flaked coconut
14-oz. can sweetened
   condensed milk

2 t. vanilla extract

Mix ingredients well in a large bowl. Drop by teaspoonfuls one inch apart on well-greased baking sheets. Press down slightly; bake at 350 degrees for 10 to 12 minutes. Immediately remove from baking sheets; let cool on a wire rack. Store loosely covered at room temperature. Makes 4 dozen.

Wassail

Sarah Lopez
Jacksonville, FL

Warm, spiced cider...so delicious!

1 gal. apple cider
2 t. whole cloves
2 t. whole allspice

2 sticks cinnamon
2/3 c. sugar

Combine all ingredients in a saucepan; bring to a boil. Reduce to low heat and simmer for 20 minutes. Strain; pour into a punch bowl to serve. Makes 32 servings.

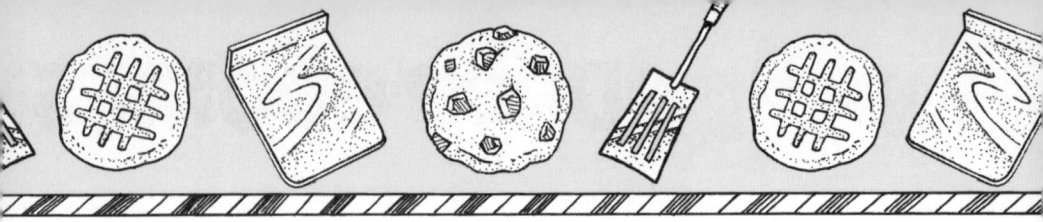

Lebkuchen

Elaine Myers
Fillmore, IN

Translated, Lebkuchen means "gingerbread," although lots of versions have no ginger in them at all...like this one. It is, however, an easy-to-make honey cookie everyone will love!

4 c. honey
11 c. all-purpose flour, divided
6 eggs
2-1/2 c. sugar
2 T. cinnamon
1 T. ground cloves

1 t. allspice
1 T. ground nutmeg
2 T. lemon juice
1 T. baking soda
Garnish: powdered sugar
    frosting, whole almonds

Warm honey in a saucepan until thin; place in a very large mixing bowl. Stir in 6-1/4 cups flour; set aside. Beat eggs until light and thick; add sugar and beat well. Stir in spices. Mix lemon juice and baking soda; stir into mixture. Add remaining flour; cover and chill. Drop by tablespoonfuls onto lightly greased baking sheets. Bake at 350 degrees for 8 to 10 minutes. When cool, frost cookies and press one almond onto each. Store in an airtight container. Makes 14 to 16 dozen.

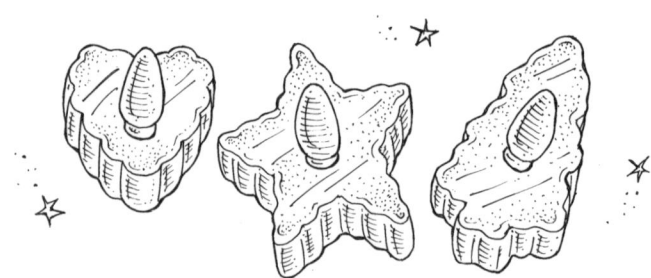

Keep cookies sweet and petite...use mini cookie cutters
or small scoops to make cookies bite-size.
Each one will be a perfect little treat so
friends & family can try one of each variety!

Orange Cookies

DeeAnn Portra
Turtle Lake, ND

*My Grandma used to bake these at Christmas. She was
a great cook and a very special lady.*

1-1/2 c. brown sugar, packed
3/4 c. butter, softened
2 eggs
1 t. vanilla extract
1-1/2 t. orange zest
1/2 c. milk

1-1/2 t. vinegar
3 c. all-purpose flour
1/4 t. salt
1-1/2 t. baking powder
1/2 t. baking soda
Optional: 3/4 c. chopped walnuts

Combine brown sugar, butter, eggs, vanilla and zest, blending after
each addition. Set aside. Mix together milk and vinegar; stir to blend
and add to brown sugar mixture. Set aside. Combine flour, salt, baking
powder and baking soda; blend well and add to brown sugar mixture.
Stir in walnuts, if using. Drop by teaspoonfuls onto greased baking
sheets. Bake for 8 to 10 minutes at 350 degrees. Frost with Orange
Frosting when cool. Makes 3 to 4 dozen.

Orange Frosting:

1/3 c. orange juice
1 c. powdered sugar

1-1/2 t. orange zest

Combine all ingredients; mix well.

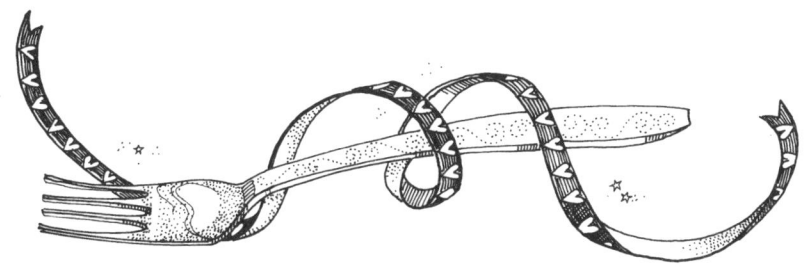

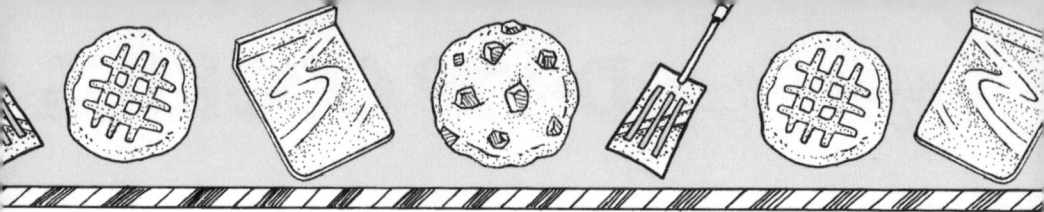

Chocolatey Pumpkin Cookies

Susan Whitney
Fountain Valley, CA

Pumpkin and chocolate go together beautifully!

1 c. shortening
1 c. sugar
1 c. canned pumpkin
1 egg
1 t. vanilla extract
2 c. all-purpose flour

1 t. baking soda
1 t. cinnamon
1/2 t. salt
3/4 c. semi-sweet
    chocolate chips

Blend together shortening, sugar, pumpkin, egg and vanilla; set aside. Sift together flour, baking soda, cinnamon and salt; stir into shortening mixture. Fold in chocolate chips. Drop by tablespoonfuls onto ungreased baking sheet. Bake at 350 degrees for 10 to 12 minutes. Frost cookies when cool. Makes 2 to 3 dozen.

Frosting:

3 T. butter
3 T. milk

1/2 c. brown sugar, packed
1-1/2 to 2 c. powdered sugar

Combine butter, milk and brown sugar in a small saucepan. Boil for 2 minutes; add enough powdered sugar to make a spreading consistency. Mix well.

For a lunchbox surprise, slip cookies inside a vellum envelope and tie closed with shoestring licorice!

Fruit Jewel Cookies

Tammy Thomas
Franklin, PA

Every Christmas is made more special by including these cookies in our baking tradition. My mother has made them every year for the holidays and I always think of her when I bake them.

1/2 c. butter, softened
1/2 c. powdered sugar
1 egg, separated
1/4 c. pineapple preserves
1 t. orange zest
1 t. vanilla extract

1 c. all-purpose flour
1/4 t. salt
1 c. finely chopped pecans
Garnish: candied cherries,
  halved

Blend butter and powdered sugar together until light and fluffy. Stir in egg yolk, preserves, zest and vanilla. Add flour and salt; mix well. Chill for 2 hours. Roll into one-inch balls; dip in beaten egg white, then into chopped pecans. Place on ungreased baking sheets; bake at 350 degrees for 10 minutes. Remove from oven; lightly press a candied cherry half into the top of each cookie. Makes 1-1/2 dozen.

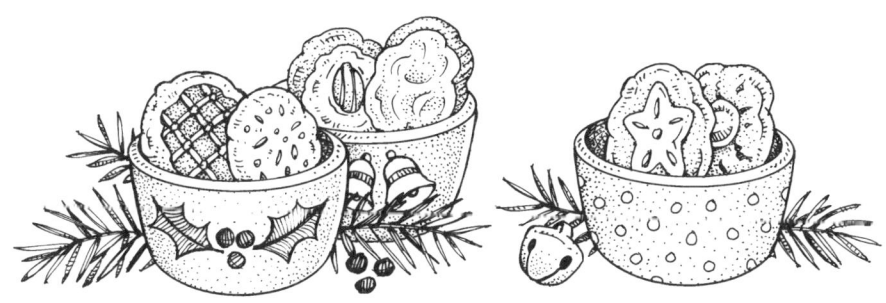

At dessert time, serve several cookies inside colorful vintage dessert cups...little elves are sure to love 'em!

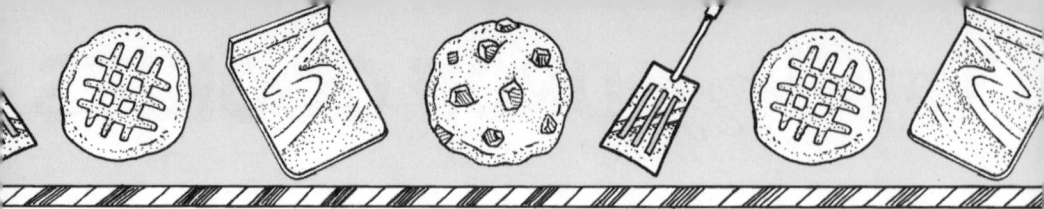

Caramel Apple Cookies

Nichole Martelli
Alvin, TX

You'll be in heaven with just one bite of these rich cookies.

1/2 c. shortening
1-1/4 c. light brown sugar,
   packed
1 egg
1/2 c. apple juice, divided
2-1/4 c. all-purpose flour
1 t. baking soda

1/4 t. salt
1 t. cinnamon
1/4 t. ground cloves
1 c. apples, cored, peeled
   and shredded
Garnish: 5 T. walnuts,
   finely chopped

Blend together shortening and brown sugar; beat in egg and 1/4 cup apple juice. Set aside. Combine flour, baking soda, salt and spices; add to shortening mixture along with remaining apple juice and apples. Drop by teaspoonfuls, 2 inches apart, onto greased baking sheets. Bake at 350 degrees for 10 to 12 minutes, until golden. Let cool on wire racks. Spread with Brown Sugar Frosting; sprinkle with chopped walnuts. Makes 2 dozen.

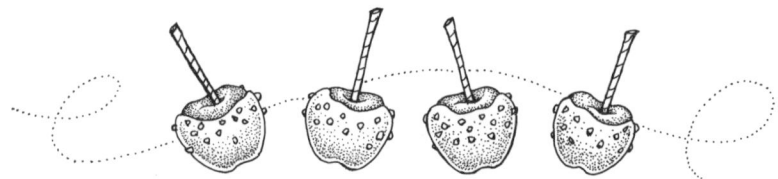

Brown Sugar Frosting:

2 to 3 T. margarine, softened
1/3 c. light brown sugar, packed
2 T. water

1-1/2 c. powdered sugar
2 to 4 T. milk

Combine margarine, brown sugar and water in a saucepan over medium-high heat, stirring until sugar dissolves. Remove from heat; stir in powdered sugar and enough milk to make a spreadable consistency. Use immediately. If frosting begins to harden, return to low heat and stir in more milk.

Razzle-Dazzle DROP COOKIES

Gingersnaps

Carol McKinney
Poulsbo, WA

My mother told me many times when she and Daddy were first married she would make these cookies. Daddy would start eating them warm from the oven until he couldn't eat any more!

1-1/2 c. shortening
2-1/2 c. sugar, divided
2 eggs
1/2 c. molasses
4 c. all-purpose flour

2 t. baking soda
2 t. cinnamon
2 t. ground cloves
2 t. ground ginger

Blend together shortening and 2 cups sugar. Mix in eggs; add molasses and set aside. Sift together flour, baking soda and spices; add to shortening mixture and blend well. Roll into one-inch balls; roll in remaining sugar. Place 2 inches apart on baking sheets lined with parchment paper. Bake at 375 degrees for 15 to 18 minutes, watching carefully toward end of baking time. Makes about 5 dozen cookies.

There's nothing like a cookie jar full of cookies, and kids away at college will be thrilled to open a care package and find one filled with Mom's best goodies.

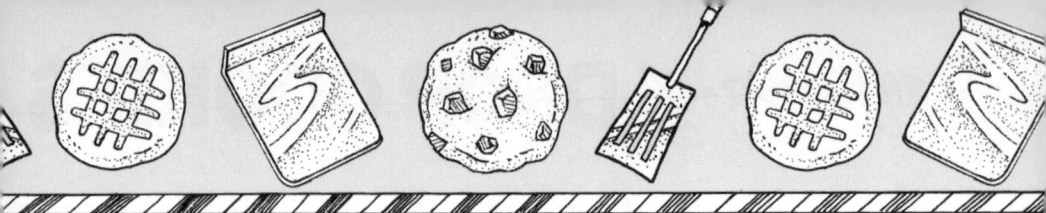

Buttery Mint Cookies

Michelle Campen
Peoria, IL

These cookies are a hit with kids of all ages! In springtime, use pastel sugars, red and blue in the summer or orange and black in the fall. These cookies always make nice gifts to give too.

3/4 c. butter
1/2 c. sugar
1 egg yolk
2 T. milk

1/4 t. mint extract
2 c. all-purpose flour
red and green colored sugars

In a mixing bowl, beat butter with an electric mixer on medium speed for 30 seconds. Add sugar; beat until combined. Beat in egg yolk, milk and extract. Add flour; blend in as much as possible with mixer. Stir in remaining flour with a wooden spoon. Cover and chill for 2 hours, or until easy to handle. Shape dough into one-inch balls; arrange on ungreased baking sheets. Dip the bottom of a glass tumbler into colored sugar and use to flatten cookies. Bake at 350 degrees for 8 to 10 minutes, or until edges begin to turn golden. Cool cookies on a wire rack. Store in an airtight container. Makes 3-1/2 dozen cookies.

Serve up cookies stacked in old-fashioned sundae glasses...what a fun after-dinner treat.

Chocolate-Peppermint Cookies

Barb Thorsen
Maple Grove, MN

The peppermint chocolate in the center of these cookies makes them irresistible!

4 1-oz. sqs. unsweetened
   baking chocolate, chopped
1 T. plus 1 t. butter, sliced
1-1/2 c. all-purpose flour
1/2 c. baking cocoa
2 t. baking powder
1/4 t. salt

4 eggs
2 c. sugar
1 t. vanilla
2 c. peppermint melting
   chocolate, chopped
Garnish: powdered sugar

Melt chocolate and butter together over low heat in a small saucepan; set aside. Stir together flour, cocoa, baking powder and salt; set aside. Combine eggs, sugar and vanilla. Mix for about 3 minutes; add chocolate mixture, then flour mixture. Mix well; cover and refrigerate for 2 hours. Shape into balls by tablespoonfuls; place 3 inches apart on parchment paper-covered baking sheets. Press 3 to 4 pieces of peppermint melting chocolate into each cookie. Bake at 325 degrees for 13 to 17 minutes. Sprinkle with powdered sugar; let cool. Makes 2-1/2 dozen.

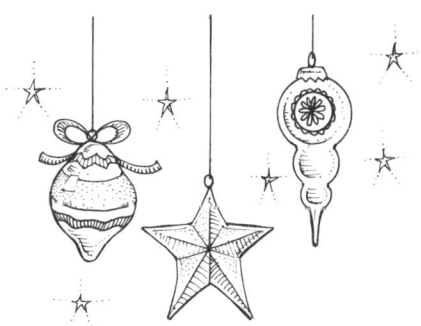

In the end, what affects your life most deeply are the things too simple to talk about.

-Neil Blane

Terrific "To"
"From" Tags in no
time! Just copy,
cut & color!

Baked with LOVE:

From the Kitchen of:

↑ Cut, color & fold in half
for an extra special tag.

A Blizzard of
BAR COOKIES

Fudge Nut Bars

Nancy Molldrem
Eau Claire, WI

When we had a neighborhood backyard potluck, my neighbor made these bar cookies...they were a hit!

1 c. butter, softened
2 c. light brown sugar, packed
2 eggs
2 t. vanilla extract
2 c. all-purpose flour

1 t. baking soda
1 t. salt
3 c. long-cooking oats, uncooked

Blend together butter and sugar; mix in eggs and vanilla and set aside. Sift together flour, baking soda and salt; stir in oats. Add flour mixture to butter mixture; mix well. Spread two-thirds of mixture in a greased jelly-roll pan; cover with Chocolate Filling. Dot with remaining one-third of mixture; swirl over filling. Bake at 350 degrees for 25 to 30 minutes; cut into 2"x1" bars. Makes 5 dozen.

Chocolate Filling:

12-oz. pkg. semi-sweet
   chocolate chips
1 c. sweetened condensed milk
2 T. butter

1/2 t. salt
2 t. vanilla extract
1 c. chopped nuts

In a saucepan over boiling water, mix together chocolate chips, condensed milk, butter and salt; stir until smooth. Stir in vanilla and nuts.

A Blizzard of **BAR COOKIES**

Chocolate Chip Bar Cookies

Lori Hibbard
Fort Wayne, IN

These moist cookies are low in sugar...shhh, don't tell anyone!

1/2 c. butter, softened
1/2 c. light brown sugar, packed
1 egg
1 banana, mashed
1-1/2 c. all-purpose flour

1/2 t. baking soda
1/2 t. baking powder
2/3 c. mini semi-sweet
   chocolate chips
1/4 c. chopped walnuts

Blend together butter, sugar, egg and banana until smooth. Add flour, baking soda and baking powder; mix well. Stir in chocolate chips and walnuts. Spread evenly in a lightly greased 13"x9" baking pan. Bake at 350 degrees for 15 minutes or until golden. Cut into bars. Makes 2-1/2 to 3 dozen.

Marshmallow Creme Frosting

Regina Vining
Warwick, RI

Use this frosting for sandwiching cookies together...yum!

1-1/3 c. margarine, softened
7-oz. jar marshmallow creme
1 T. vanilla extract

1 t. almond extract
1 to 1-1/2 t. milk
2-2/3 c. powdered sugar

Blend margarine and marshmallow creme together until smooth; add extracts and milk and mix well. Beat in powdered sugar with an electric mixer on medium speed until smooth. Makes 3 cups.

Goodies to go...top bar cookies with frosting, then add green chocolate-covered candies in a tree or wreath shape. Fun treats for a school holiday party!

Maple Syrup Shortbread

Karen Donker
Alliance, NE

The flavor of maple paired with walnuts turns these into a real treat.

1/2 c. plus 1 T. butter, softened
   and divided
1/4 c. sugar
1 c. all-purpose flour
3/4 c. brown sugar, packed

1/2 c. maple syrup
1 egg
1 t. vanilla extract
Optional: 1/2 c. chopped walnuts

Blend 1/2 cup butter and sugar together in a large bowl until light and fluffy. Add flour a little at a time, mixing continually; blend well. Pat mixture into a lightly greased 8"x8" baking pan. Bake at 350 degrees until light golden, about 25 minutes; remove from oven and set aside. Stir together brown sugar, syrup and remaining butter. Add egg and vanilla; mix until smooth. Pour evenly over baked shortbread; sprinkle with walnuts. Return to oven; bake at 350 degrees until topping sets, about 20 minutes. Let cool; cut into 1-1/2"x1-1/2" squares. Store in an airtight container. Makes about 1-1/2 dozen.

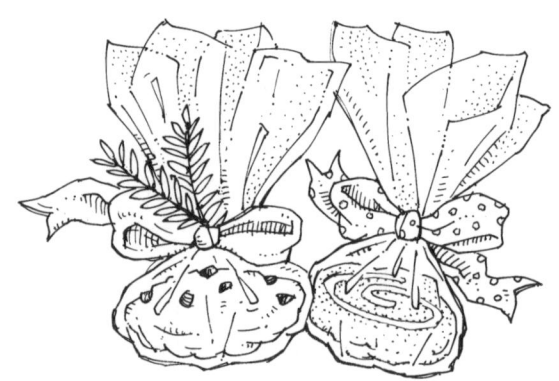

Think outside the box...wrap cookies in clear or colored cellophane for gift giving. Tied up with a bow or curly ribbon, it's festive...fast!

A Blizzard of BAR COOKIES

Date-Nut Cookie Bars

Elizabeth Lynch
Schiller Park, IL

Sometimes I toss dried cranberries into the dough...great!

2 eggs
1/2 c. sugar
1/2 t. vanilla extract
1/2 c. all-purpose flour
1/2 t. salt

1/2 t. baking powder
1 c. walnuts
2 c. chopped dates
Garnish: powdered sugar

Beat eggs until foamy; add sugar and vanilla. Sift together flour, salt, and baking powder; stir into egg mixture. Mix in walnuts and dates; spread in a well greased 9"x9" pan. Bake at 325 degrees for 25 to 30 minutes. Cut into small squares and sprinkle with powdered sugar. Makes 1-1/2 to 2 dozen.

Hot Cocoa Nog

Leah Finks
Delaware, OH

Deliciously different...chocolatey eggnog.

2 qts. eggnog
16-oz. can chocolate syrup
Optional: 1/2 c. light rum

1 c. whipping cream
2 T. powdered sugar
Garnish: baking cocoa

Combine eggnog, chocolate syrup and rum, if desired, in a large punch bowl, stirring well. In a separate bowl, beat whipping cream with an electric mixer at high speed until foamy. Add powdered sugar and continue beating until stiff peaks form. Dollop whipped cream over eggnog; sift cocoa over top. Serve immediately. Makes 3 quarts.

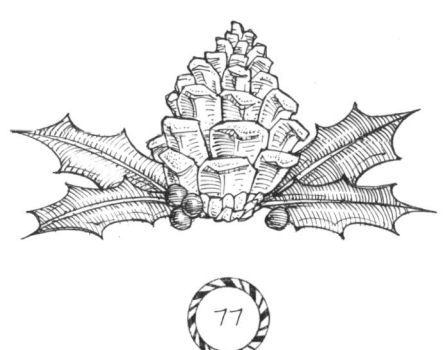

Lemon-Oatmeal Bars

Carrie Kiiskila
Racine, WI

The tangy taste of lemon and orange is so refreshing.

1 c. butter, softened
1 c. sugar
2 c. all-purpose flour
1-1/4 c. long-cooking oats,
   uncooked

juice and zest of 2 lemons
juice and zest of 1 orange
14-oz. can sweetened
   condensed milk

Blend together butter and sugar. Stir in flour and oats to make a crumbly dough. Press two-thirds of dough into a greased 13"x9" baking pan; set aside. Stir juices and zests into condensed milk; spread evenly over dough in pan. Sprinkle remaining dough over top. Bake at 350 degrees for 30 to 35 minutes or until golden. When cool, cut into 2"x2" squares. Makes 2-1/2 to 3 dozen.

Here's a cookie swap table tent with a holiday feel...jot the cookie name on a piece of cardstock, then tuck the card into a pinecone.

A Blizzard of BAR COOKIES

Cream Cheese Bar Cookies

*Amy Prather
Longview, WA*

My mother-in-law always made these delicious cookies...now I'm carrying on the tradition.

1 c. butter, softened
1/2 c. sugar
1/2 c. cornstarch
2-1/4 c. all-purpose flour
4 eggs

16-oz. pkg. brown sugar
1/2 t. baking powder
2 t. vanilla extract
1/2 c. chopped walnuts
1/2 c. flaked coconut

Blend butter, sugar, cornstarch and 2 cups flour with a pastry blender. Pat into an ungreased jelly-roll pan; bake for 15 minutes at 350 degrees. Combine eggs, brown sugar, remaining flour, baking powder, vanilla, nuts and coconut; mix well and spread on baked layer. Bake at 350 degrees for 30 minutes. Let cool; spread with Cream Cheese Topping. Cut into bars. Makes 3-1/2 to 4 dozen.

Cream Cheese Topping:

8-oz. pkg. cream cheese, softened
1/2 c. softened butter

16-oz. pkg. powdered sugar
1 t. vanilla extract

Combine all ingredients; mix well.

Turn a simple pencil box into a sweet gift box. Covered with festive trims like colorful paper, ribbon, chenille rick-rack or buttons, in no time it's ready to fill with homebaked goodies!

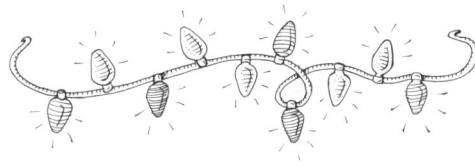

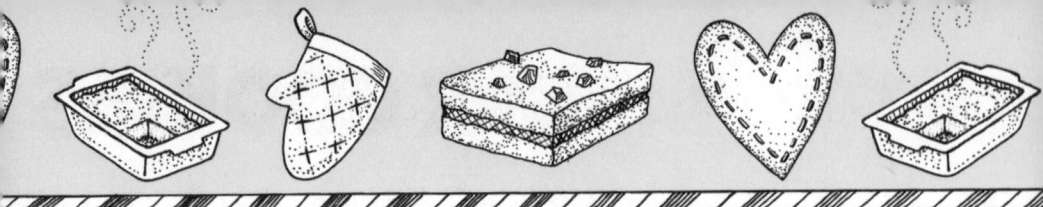

Christmas Fruit Bars

Dana Irish
Pflugerville, TX

These bar cookies have been one of my favorites since I was a kid.
They're easy to make and very pretty too!

1/2 c. shortening
1-1/3 c. brown sugar, packed
1/2 t. cinnamon
1/4 t. ground cloves
1/4 t. nutmeg
2 eggs

1-1/2 c. all-purpose flour
1 t. salt
1/2 t. baking soda
2 c. candied fruit, chopped
1 c. chopped nuts

Blend together shortening, brown sugar and spices until fluffy.
Stir in eggs; set aside. Sift together flour, salt and baking soda; add to
shortening mixture. Spread evenly in a greased 13"x9" baking pan;
sprinkle fruit and nuts evenly over top. Bake at 350 degrees for
25 minutes. Cut into bars. Makes 2-1/2 to 3 dozen.

Goodies look even more special when they're given
wrapped with care. It's easy to use fabric glue to
add simple snowflakes (cut from white felt)
onto a blue tea towel...so sweet!

Peanut Butter Swirl Bars

Char Nix
Tustin, MI

Pairing up chocolate and peanut butter is a very good thing!

1/2 c. creamy peanut butter
1/3 c. butter, softened
3/4 c. sugar
3/4 c. brown sugar, packed
2 eggs

2 t. vanilla extract
1 c. all-purpose flour
1 t. baking powder
12-oz. pkg. semi-sweet
    chocolate chips

Blend together peanut butter, butter and sugars until creamy; add eggs and vanilla. Stir in flour and baking powder; mix well. Spread in a greased 13"x9" baking pan; top with chocolate chips. Bake at 350 degrees for 5 minutes. Remove from oven; run a knife through batter to marbleize. Return to oven for an additional 30 minutes at 350 degrees. Cut into bars. Makes 2-1/2 to 3 dozen.

Easy Vanilla Frosting

Jo Ann
Gooseberry Patch

So simple, let the kids help.

2 T. egg substitute
1 c. corn syrup

1 t. vanilla extract

Combine all ingredients in a mixing bowl; beat with an electric mixer on high speed for 6 to 7 minutes. Makes 3 cups.

Search out flea markets for tin cones to fill with sweet treats. Surprise a friend by slipping one on her door knob or add a ribbon to the cone and loop on a chair back for a clever party favor.

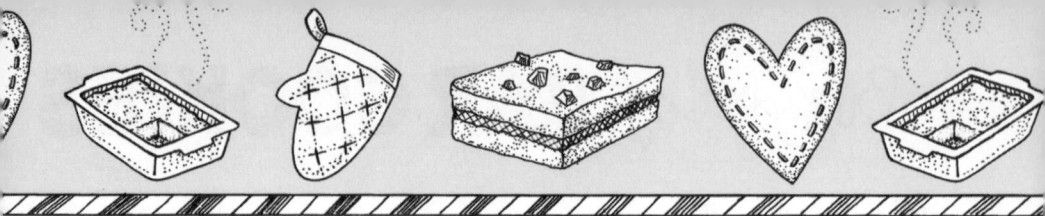

Chocolate-Butterscotch Bars

Debbie Isaacson
Irvine, CA

These cookies were made by my mother for every family get-together, and would disappear in minutes!

12-oz. pkg. semi-sweet
   chocolate chips
12-oz. pkg. butterscotch chips
1 c. creamy peanut butter

16-oz. pkg. mini marshmallows
1 t. vanilla extract
1 c. Spanish peanuts
2 c. crispy rice cereal

Melt together chocolate chips, butterscotch chips and peanut butter in a large saucepan over low heat. Stir in marshmallows, vanilla, peanuts and cereal. Pour into 2 greased 8"x8" baking pans or one greased 13"x9" baking pan; press down firmly and evenly. Chill until set; cut into small squares. Makes 2-1/2 to 3 dozen.

Cookies can be stored and still keep their just-baked-taste for up to two weeks. Just remember to keep them airtight...plastic zipping bags or containers with tight-fitting lids are perfect. Even Grandma's cookie jar will keep cookies delicious as long as the lid is on securely.

Chocolate-Cherry Bars

Maylene Anderson
Webster City, IA

What could possibly be better than chocolate and cherries? Make these bars to share with friends, but keep a few for yourself too.

18-1/2 oz. pkg. devil's food
   cake mix

21-oz. can cherry pie filling
1 t. almond extract

Mix together all ingredients; spread in a greased 13"x9" baking pan. Bake at 350 degrees for about 25 to 35 minutes, until top springs back when touched. Spread with Chocolate Frosting while still warm; cut into bars. Makes 2-1/2 to 3 dozen.

Chocolate Frosting:

1 c. sugar
1/3 c. milk

5 T. margarine
1 c. semi-sweet chocolate chips

Combine sugar, milk and margarine in a saucepan. Bring to a boil; boil for one minute, stirring constantly. Remove from heat; stir in chocolate chips until melted.

Cookie clean-up is a snap for bar cookies...just line the baking pan with aluminum foil before adding the dough. Once the cookies have completely cooled, lift the cookies out, peel off the foil and cut into bars.

Eggnog Bars

Lorraine Caland
Ontario, Canada

Whenever we share these with friends, they always ask to take a few home. And more often than not, the recipe goes along too.

1/2 c. butter, softened
1 c. sugar
1 t. rum extract
2-1/4 c. all-purpose flour
1 t. baking soda

1/4 t. nutmeg
1/8 t. salt
1 c. eggnog
1 c. maraschino cherries, chopped

Blend together butter and sugar until fluffy; blend in extract and set aside. Combine flour, baking soda, nutmeg and salt. Add flour mixture alternately with eggnog to butter mixture; stir in cherries. Spread in a greased jelly-roll pan. Bake at 350 degrees for 18 to 20 minutes, testing for doneness with a toothpick. Drizzle with frosting while still warm. Let cool; cut into bars. Makes 4 dozen.

Frosting:

3/4 c. powdered sugar
1/2 t. rum extract
3 to 4 t. milk

Optional: several drops food coloring

Mix all ingredients together until smooth.

Variety is easy in cookie recipes. Finely chopped hazelnuts or macadamia nuts are a tasty substitution for walnuts in a favorite recipe.

A Blizzard of **BAR COOKIES**

Applesauce Spice Bars

Barbara Wise
Jamestown, OH

*I found this recipe over 35 years ago on the back of a flour bag.
These are the cookies my family insists I make whenever
we have a family get-together.*

1 c. all-purpose flour
2/3 c. brown sugar, packed
1 t. baking soda
1/2 t. salt
1 t. pumpkin pie spice

1/4 c. shortening
1 c. applesauce
1 egg
Optional: 1 c. raisins

Combine all ingredients; mix thoroughly. Spread in a greased
13"x9" baking pan. Bake for about 25 minutes at 350 degrees.
Let cool; frost with Browned Butter Frosting. Cut into 3"x1" bars.
Makes 2-1/2 to 3 dozen.

Browned Butter Frosting:

3 T. butter
1-1/2 c. powdered sugar

1 t. vanilla extract
1 to 1-1/2 T. milk

Heat butter in a saucepan over medium heat until it turns a delicate
brown; remove from heat. Blend in remaining ingredients; beat until
frosting is smooth and a spreading consistency.

*A budding baker will
squeal with delight to receive
an apron with pockets filled
to the brim with cookie
cutters, jimmies, glittery
sugars, frostings and
tried & true recipes.*

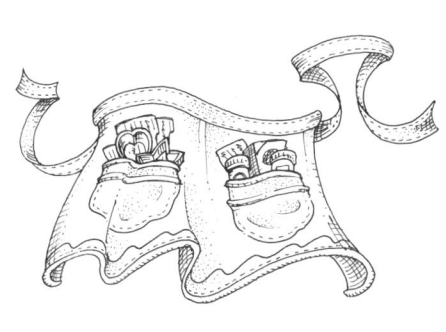

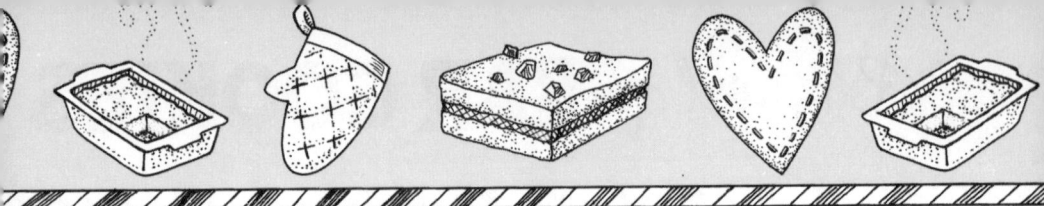

Double Bars

Julie Milliken
Lakewood, CO

All the yummy goodies in these layered bars are found in one bite.

1/2 c. margarine
1-1/2 c. graham cracker crumbs
14-oz. can sweetened
    condensed milk

12-oz. pkg. semi-sweet
    chocolate chips
1 c. peanut butter chips

Melt margarine in a 13"x9" baking pan. Spread crumbs evenly over margarine; spread condensed milk evenly over crumbs. Top with chocolate and peanut butter chips; press down firmly. Bake at 350 degrees for 25 to 30 minutes; let cool for 5 minutes and cut into bars. Makes 2-1/2 to 3 dozen.

Here are some simple high-altitude cookie baking hints: If you're above 3000 feet, decrease the baking temperature by 25 degrees and reduce the amount of sugar by 2 tablespoons per cup. If you live over 5000 feet, follow the suggestions above and also decrease the baking powder a recipe calls for by one-half.

Pumpkin Squares

Kelly Liggett
Grand Haven, MI

*Don't think of pumpkin as a fall-only treat...these are
a hit year 'round.*

4 eggs	1 t. baking powder
1 c. oil	1 t. baking soda
2 c. sugar	2 t. cinnamon
1-1/2 c. pumpkin	2 c. all-purpose flour
1/2 t. salt	

Mix all ingredients together; pour into a greased jelly-roll pan. Bake at 350 degrees for 25 minutes. Cool and frost. Refrigerate for one hour before serving. Makes 3-1/2 to 4 dozen.

Frosting:

8-oz. pkg. cream cheese, softened	1-1/2 c. powdered sugar
	2 t. vanilla extract
1/2 c. plus 2 T. margarine	2 t. milk

Blend all ingredients together with an electric mixer on medium speed until smooth.

Arrange lots of yummy bar cookies on a vintage pie plate, then tie up with tulle. So pretty!

Nutmeg Squares

Debbie Reina
Houston, TX

I've been known to call my friend Nancy asking, "Do you have the nutmeg recipe? I can't find mine!" Sure enough, she does. We both simply love this crunchy cookie!

1 c. butter, softened
1 c. sugar
2 c. all-purpose flour

1-1/2 t. nutmeg
1 egg, separated

Combine butter, sugar, flour, nutmeg and egg yolk. Mix well, using hands if necessary. Pat into an ungreased jelly-roll pan; beat egg white and brush over top. Bake for one hour at 275 degrees. Let cool; cut into squares. Makes 3-1/2 to 4 dozen.

Allspice-Cream Cheese Frosting

Anna Pindell
Herrod, OH

Yum...perfect for spicy cookies.

3-oz. pkg. cream cheese
1/3 c. butter, softened
3/4 t. allspice

4 c. powdered sugar
1 t. vanilla extract
2 T. milk

Beat cream cheese, butter and allspice in a bowl with an electric mixer on medium speed until blended. Gradually add powdered sugar and blend until well combined. Stir in vanilla; gradually add milk, beating until frosting is of spreading consistency. Makes 3 cups.

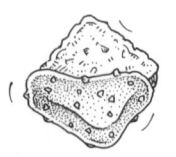

Who says bar cookies can't have some extra pizazz? Dip them halfway into melted chocolate, then sprinkle with nuts or mini chips.

Peanut Butter Whimsy Bars

*Erin States
Springville, PA*

The kids love these after school, after play...anytime!

2 c. sugar
1/2 c. milk
1/2 c. butter
1/8 t. salt

1 t. vanilla
1/2 c. creamy peanut butter
3 c. quick-cooking oats,
    uncooked

Combine sugar, milk, butter and salt in a saucepan; bring to a boil. Boil for one minute; remove from heat. Add vanilla and peanut butter; stir until smooth. Pour over oats in a large mixing bowl; mix well. Pour mixture into a 13"x9" baking pan lined with wax paper. Allow to cool completely. Lift wax paper out of pan; cut into squares. Makes 2-1/2 to 3 dozen.

An oversize mug is perfect for filling with cookies or candy...what a terrific surprise for friends at the office!

Chinese Chews

Elaine Nichols
Mesa, AZ

While I was growing up, Mom baked these all the time. I remember
they were so delicious with a glass of milk. Now as an adult,
I still enjoy them.

1/2 c. shortening
1 c. sugar
2 eggs, separated
1 t. vanilla extract
1-1/2 c. all-purpose flour

1 t. baking powder
1/2 t. salt
1 c. semi-sweet chocolate chips
1 c. brown sugar, packed

Blend together shortening and sugar. Add egg yolks and vanilla; mix
well. Add flour, baking powder and salt; mix thoroughly. Press into the
bottom of a greased 13"x9" baking pan. Sprinkle with chocolate chips;
press down lightly and set aside. Beat egg whites with an electric
mixer until fluffy. Gradually add brown sugar; continue beating until
soft peaks form. Spread egg white mixture evenly over chocolate chips.
Bake at 350 degrees for 25 minutes. Let cool completely; cut into bars.
Makes 2 dozen.

Give a cookie sampler! Just use poster board to divide
a round cookie tin into equal sections. Fill each with
a different cookie or candy...a hit!

A Blizzard of BAR COOKIES

Chocolate-Honey Squares

Jennifer Eveland-Kupp
Temple, PA

Sure to be a hit at any gathering!

1/3 c. butter
1/2 c. baking cocoa
1/3 c. honey
3 c. mini marshmallows

1 t. vanilla extract
4 c. crispy rice cereal
1 c. peanuts

Melt butter in a large saucepan; blend in cocoa, honey and marshmallows. Cook over low heat, stirring constantly until smooth and marshmallows are melted. Remove from heat; stir in vanilla, cereal and peanuts until coated. Press lightly into a greased 9"x9" baking pan. Cut into squares when cooled. Makes 1-1/2 to 2 dozen.

Keep in mind that bar cookie dough should always
be baked in the pan size the recipe calls for.
If a larger pan size is used, the cookies will be dry.
If the pan is too small the cookies will be underbaked.

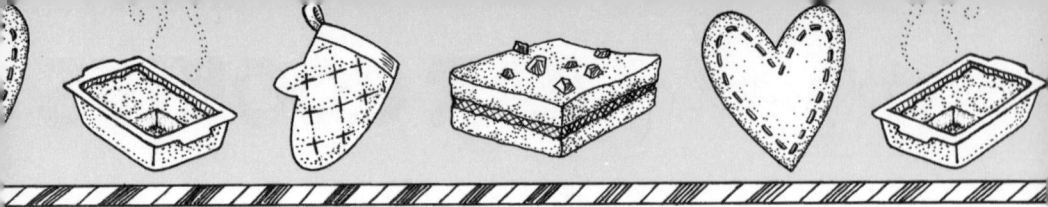

Double-Chocolate Brownies

Liz Gist
Orlando, FL

You can't stop with just one!

3 1-oz. sqs. unsweetened
   baking chocolate
6 T. butter
2/3 c. all-purpose flour
1/8 t. salt

1-1/3 c. sugar
3 eggs, beaten
1 t. vanilla extract
3/4 c. semi-sweet
   chocolate chips

Melt together unsweetened chocolate and butter in a small, heavy saucepan over low heat. Stir until smooth; remove from heat and let cool slightly. Stir together flour and salt; set aside. Gradually stir sugar into cooled chocolate mixture. Add eggs and vanilla; stir just to combine. Fold in flour mixture. Spread in an 8"x8" baking pan sprayed with non-stick vegetable spray. Sprinkle with chocolate chips; bake at 325 degrees for 30 to 35 minutes. Use a knife to spread melted chips over the surface. Let cool; cut into squares. Makes one dozen.

Just for fun, cut brownies with a round cookie cutter and stack inside an old-fashioned canning jar.

Nana's Buttermilk Brownies

Brenda Berby
Northborough, MA

Friends will love the rich taste of real homemade brownies.

1 c. margarine	1 t. baking soda
1 c. water	1/2 t. salt
1/3 c. baking cocoa	1/2 c. buttermilk
2 c. all-purpose flour	2 eggs, beaten
2 c. sugar	1-1/2 t. vanilla extract

In a saucepan, combine margarine, water and cocoa; cook until mixture comes to a boil. Remove from heat; set aside. In a bowl, stir together flour, sugar, baking soda and salt; add buttermilk, eggs and vanilla. Pour into margarine mixture; beat until well combined. Pour into a greased and floured jelly-roll pan; bake at 400 degrees for 20 minutes. Spread Chocolate-Buttermilk Frosting over the top; cut into large squares. Makes 2 dozen.

Chocolate-Buttermilk Frosting:

4 T. butter	1 t. vanilla extract
1/4 c. baking cocoa	2-1/4 c. powdered sugar
1/4 c. buttermilk	

In a saucepan, combine butter, cocoa and buttermilk; bring to a boil. Remove from heat; stir in vanilla and powdered sugar.

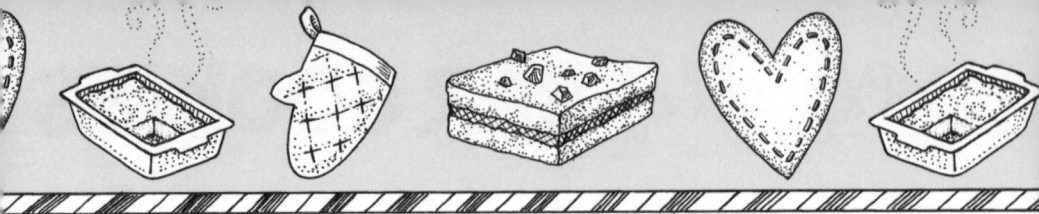

Pineapple Bars

Phyllis Peters
Three Rivers, MI

Give these mouthwatering bars on a pretty tray all wrapped in clear cellophane. Tie with a bow and add a tag...the perfect hostess gift.

2 eggs, beaten
1-1/2 c. sugar
1 t. vanilla extract
20-oz. can crushed pineapple,
   juice reserved

2-1/4 c. all-purpose flour
1-1/2 t. baking soda
Optional: 1-1/2 c. flaked
   coconut, 1/2 c. English
   walnuts, broken up

Combine eggs, sugar and vanilla; stir in pineapple with juice, flour and baking soda, coconut and walnuts, if using. Pour into a greased jelly-roll pan; bake at 350 degrees for 20 to 25 minutes. Spread Vanilla Glaze over top while still warm; cut into bars. Makes 3 to 3-1/2 dozen.

Vanilla Glaze:

3/4 c. sugar
1/4 c. evaporated milk

1/2 c. margarine
1 t. vanilla extract

Mix all ingredients together; bring to a boil. Cook for 30 seconds.

Jams and jellies add a yummy tartness to cookies. Sandwich jam between two cookies or warm it for a simple fruity glaze.

Banana Split Bars

Carol Hickman
Kingsport, TN

The flavor of an all-time favorite dessert in a cookie!

1/3 c. butter, softened
1 c. sugar
1 egg
1 banana, mashed
1 t. vanilla extract
1-1/4 c. all-purpose flour
1 t. baking powder

1/4 t. salt
1/3 c. chopped walnuts
2 c. mini marshmallows
1 c. semi-sweet chocolate chips
1/3 c. maraschino cherries,
    quartered

Stir butter and sugar together; add egg, banana and vanilla. Stir in flour, baking powder and salt; add nuts. Pour into a greased 13"x9" baking pan; bake at 350 degrees for 20 minutes. Remove from oven; sprinkle with marshmallows, chocolate chips and cherries. Bake for an additional 10 to 15 minutes; cool. Cut into bars. Makes 2 dozen.

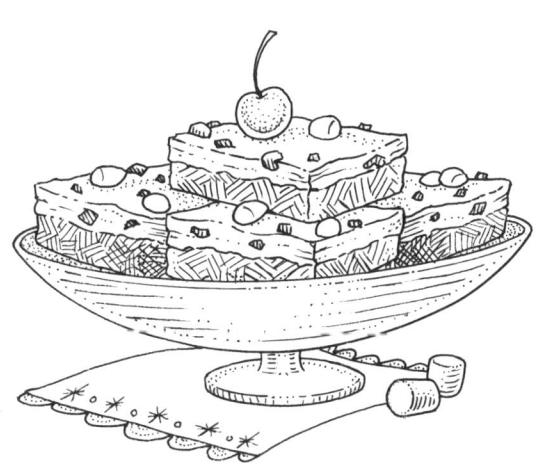

Fill a soda shop-style banana split bowl with Banana Split Bars...sure to get smiles!

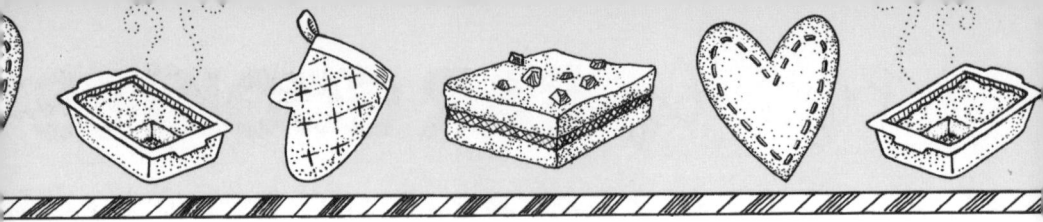

Lemon-Butter Snow Bars

Linda Hendrix
Moundville, MO

Lay a small cookie cutter over each bar before dusting with powdered sugar...so pretty.

1/2 c. butter, softened
1-1/3 c. plus 2 T. all-purpose
   flour, divided
1 c. sugar, divided
2 eggs

1/4 t. baking powder
3 T. lemon juice
1 t. lemon zest
Garnish: powdered sugar

In a medium mixing bowl, combine butter, 1-1/3 cups flour and 1/4 cup sugar. Mix on low speed for one minute with an electric mixer. Pat into an ungreased 8"x8" baking pan. Bake at 350 degrees for 15 to 20 minutes or until golden on edges. For filling, combine remaining flour, sugar, eggs, baking powder, lemon juice and lemon zest; blend well. Pour filling over partially baked crust. Bake at 350 degrees for an additional 18 to 20 minutes or until set; cool. Sprinkle with powdered sugar; cut into bars. Makes one dozen.

A lunchbox treat...pop wrapped cookies in the freezer the night before. When packing lunch in the morning, add a bag of frozen cookies to each lunchbox. They help keep the lunches cool and are ready to eat by lunchtime!

Apricot Bars

Ann Magner
New Port Richey, FL

Stack these yummy bars pyramid-style on a festive cake plate.
They won't last long.

2/3 c. dried apricots, chopped
1/2 c. butter
1/4 c. sugar
1-1/3 c. all-purpose flour,
    divided
1/2 t. baking powder

1/2 t. salt
1 c. brown sugar, packed
2 eggs
1/2 t. vanilla extract
1/2 c. chopped nuts
Garnish: powdered sugar

Cover apricots with water in a saucepan and simmer for 10 minutes; drain and set aside. Mix butter, sugar and one cup flour until crumbly. Pat into a greased 8"x8" baking pan lined with greased aluminum foil. Bake at 350 degrees for 25 minutes, or until lightly golden. Sift together remaining flour, baking powder and salt; set aside. Gradually beat brown sugar into eggs. Add flour mixture and mix well. Add vanilla, nuts and apricots. Spread over baked layer; bake an additional 30 minutes. Cool in pan; cut into squares and roll in powdered sugar. Makes one dozen.

Cookies by the pint! Fill wooden berry baskets lined with parchment paper with an assortment of cookies. Trim the paper edges with pinking shears just for zing!

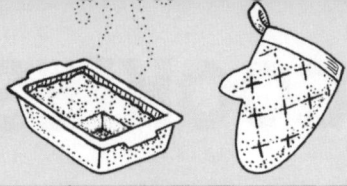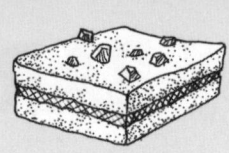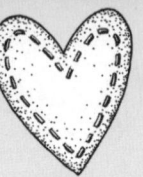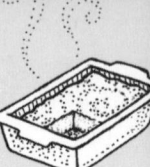

Chocolate-Caramel Bars

Camille Wheeler
Buena Vista, VA

Welcome loved ones home for the holidays with freshly baked cookies...there's nothing like this aroma as they come through the door.

1-3/4 c. plus 3 T. all-purpose
    flour, divided
1-3/4 c. quick-cooking oats,
    uncooked
1 c. brown sugar, packed
1/2 t. baking soda

1/4 t. salt
1/2 c. fruit purée for baking
1/4 c. oil
1 c. semi-sweet chocolate chips
3/4 c. caramel topping

Combine 1-3/4 cups flour, oats, brown sugar, baking soda and salt. Add fruit purée and oil; stir with fork until evenly moist and crumbly. Reserve one cup for topping. Press remaining mixture evenly into bottom of a 13"x9" pan coated with non-stick vegetable spray. Bake at 350 degrees for 15 minutes. Let cool for 10 minutes; sprinkle with chocolate chips. Stir remaining flour into caramel topping; drizzle over chocolate. Sprinkle with reserved flour mixture. Bake an additional 15 minutes or until edges are golden; cool and cut into bars. Makes 3 dozen.

Tag and yard sales can turn up retro tea and coffee tins along with vintage handkerchiefs and shiny, tinsel garlands...all great for packaging.

Scotcharoos

Kelly German
Port Angeles, WA

Practically foolproof!

1 c. corn syrup
1 c. sugar
1 c. creamy peanut butter
6 to 7 c. crispy rice cereal

12-oz. pkg. semi-sweet
chocolate chips
6-oz. pkg. butterscotch chips

In a large pan, heat corn syrup and sugar over low heat; mix until dissolved. Stir in peanut butter until melted. Remove from heat and add crispy rice cereal. Mix well and press into the bottom of a greased 13"x9" pan. Sprinkle chocolate and butterscotch chips on top. Bake at 300 degrees for approximately 5 minutes to melt chocolate; spread with knife and cool. Cut into squares. Makes 2-1/2 to 3 dozen.

Don't forget icy milk is perfect with cookies!
Some dairies still sell milk in bottles, or it can be
served up in a new vintage-style milk bottle too.
What a fun "remember when" memory.

Fudge Bars

Jane Granger
Manteno, IL

Generations of kids have loved fudge...this recipe's a winner!

1 c. margarine
2 c. brown sugar, packed
2 eggs
2 t. vanilla extract
2-1/2 c. all-purpose flour
1 t. baking soda
1 t. salt

3 c. quick-cooking oats,
  uncooked
12-oz. pkg. milk chocolate chips
14-oz. can sweetened
  condensed milk
2 T. margarine
1 c. chopped walnuts

Blend together margarine and brown sugar. Add eggs and vanilla; beat well and set aside. Mix flour, baking soda, salt and oats together. Stir in brown sugar mixture. Pat two-thirds of oat mixture in bottom of a greased jelly-roll pan. Melt together chocolate chips, sweetened condensed milk and margarine; stir in walnuts. Spread fudge filling over the oat mixture. Drop remaining one-third of oat mixture on top of the fudge layer by teaspoonfuls. Bake at 350 degrees for 25 minutes; cut into bars. Makes 3-1/2 to 4 dozen.

Need a dusting of powdered sugar on bar cookies, but don't have a small strainer? Spoon some powdered sugar into a tea infuser and give it a shake. It works like a charm!

Chocolatey Caramel-Pecan Bars

Kathy Grashoff
Fort Wayne, IN

Caramel and pecans are always a terrific twosome.

1/2 c. powdered sugar
1/2 c. butter, softened
1/3 c. plus 3 T. whipping cream,
   divided
1 c. all-purpose flour

24 caramels, unwrapped
2 c. pecan halves
1 t. margarine
1/2 c. milk chocolate chips

Combine powdered sugar, butter and one tablespoon whipping cream; blend well. Add flour; mix until crumbly. With floured hands, press evenly into a greased 9"x9" baking pan. Bake at 325 degrees for 15 to 20 minutes or until firm to the touch. In a medium saucepan, combine caramels and 1/3 cup whipping cream. Cook over low heat, stirring frequently, until caramels are melted and mixture is smooth. Remove from heat. Add pecans; stir well to coat. Immediately spoon over baked base; spread carefully to cover. In a small saucepan, over low heat, melt margarine and chocolate chips, stirring constantly. Stir in remaining whipping cream; drizzle over filling. Refrigerate one hour or until filling is firm. Cut into bars. Makes 2 dozen.

Spray the inside of liquid measuring cups with non-stick vegetable spray...it keeps sticky ingredients from clinging to the cup, making cleanup a snap.

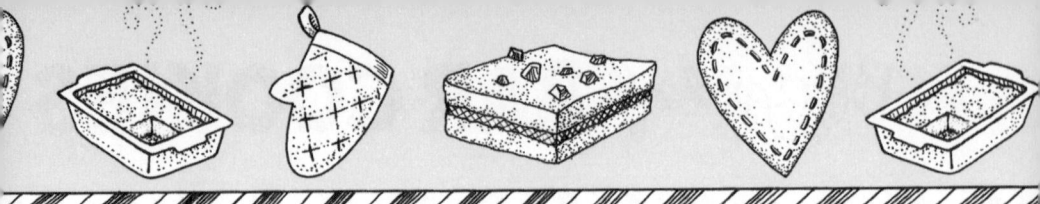

Aunt Ownie's Chocolate Bars

Wendy Lee Paffenroth
Pine Island, NY

A best-loved recipe from my husband's Aunt Eleanor.

1 c. plus 2 T. butter, divided
1/2 c. brown sugar, packed
1/2 c. sugar
2 egg yolks
1 c. all-purpose flour

1 c. quick-cooking oats,
  uncooked
10-oz. chocolate bar, chopped
1/2 c. nuts, finely chopped

Blend one cup butter and sugars together. Beat in egg yolks, flour and oats; beat well. Spread in a greased and floured 13"x9" baking pan. Bake at 350 degrees for 20 minutes; cool for 10 minutes. Melt chocolate bar with remaining butter; spread over top while warm. Sprinkle with nuts; press nuts into chocolate mixture with the back of a spoon. Cool and cut into 1"x1" bars. Makes about 4 dozen.

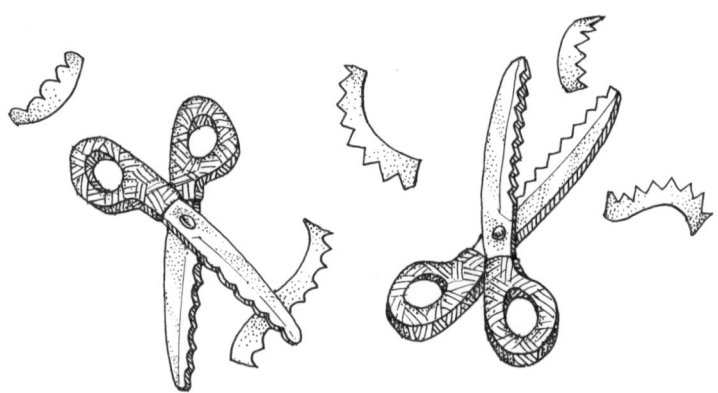

Keep a few pairs of decorative-edge scissors
on hand...terrific for adding a pretty edge
to wax, parchment or tissue paper when
wrapping up cookies to give.

A Blizzard of BAR COOKIES

Peanutty Caramel Bars

Sheila Placke
Carrollton, MO

Nothing says holidays more than trays filled with cookies that have been made with love in your own kitchen!

14-oz. pkg. caramels, unwrapped
1/4 c. water
3/4 c. creamy peanut butter, divided

4 c. doughnut-shaped oat cereal
1 c. peanuts
1 c. milk chocolate chips
1/2 c. butter, melted

Heat caramels, water and 1/2 cup peanut butter in a large saucepan until melted. Add cereal and peanuts; stir until coated. Spread into a greased 13"x9" pan. Set aside. In another pan, heat chocolate chips, butter and remaining peanut butter over low heat until melted; spread over cereal mixture. Refrigerate before cutting into bars. Makes about 3 dozen.

Photocopy family photos to use as gift tags. Just trim and secure with spray adhesive to a larger piece of cardstock. Use a hole punch in one end and slip rick-rack or a length of ribbon through the hole to tie onto a gift. A sweet tag no matter what the occasion!

To:
From:

Feel free to copy
these and use
colored pens to
give them some
ZING!

To:

From:

Snow
KIDDING

Carmelitas

Sally Derkenne
Des Moines, IA

*For a coffee-lover, pair Carmelitas with a big bag of
coffee beans and a pretty mug.*

18-oz. tube refrigerated
　chocolate chip cookie dough
6-oz. pkg. semi-sweet
　chocolate chips

32 vanilla caramels, unwrapped
1/4 c. half-and-half

Slice cookie dough 1/4-inch thick; place slices in the bottom of an
ungreased 9"x9" baking pan. Pat to make an even crust; bake at
375 degrees for 25 minutes. Let cool slightly; sprinkle with chocolate
chips and set aside. Melt caramels and half-and-half together in a
double boiler over hot water. Spread caramel mixture on top of
chocolate chips. Refrigerate for one to 2 hours; cut into squares.
Makes 3 dozen.

Cookie exchanges can be any time of year. Swap
sweet treats on Valentine's Day, chocolatey candies at
Easter or spooky shaped cut-outs on Halloween!

Peanut Butter Chipper Cookies

Tami Bowman
Marysville, OH

*Store-bought sugar cookie dough means prep time
for this recipe is only 5 minutes!*

18-oz. tube refrigerated sugar
  cookie dough
1/2 c. creamy peanut butter
1/2 c. peanut butter chips

1/2 c. semi-sweet
  chocolate chips
1/2 c. peanuts, coarsely chopped

Blend together cookie dough and peanut butter in a large bowl until
smooth. Mix in peanut butter chips, chocolate chips and nuts until
evenly distributed. Drop by heaping tablespoonfuls onto ungreased
baking sheets. Bake at 350 degrees for 15 minutes. Let cool slightly
on baking sheets; remove to wire racks and cool. Makes 2 to 3 dozen.

Kids love cookie decorating too. Set out lots of
cookies that have already been baked and cooled,
then let little ones decorate them. Arrange tubes of
frosting, jimmies, candies and sparkly sugars
on a table and let them have fun!

"Cheesecake" Cookie Cups

Tanya Graham
Lawrenceville, GA

Wonderful cheesecake taste...no one will know your secret!

12 slices refrigerated sugar
    cookie dough
8-oz. pkg. cream cheese,
    softened
1/2 c. sweetened
    condensed milk

1 egg
1 t. vanilla extract
Optional: 21-oz. can cherry
    pie filling

Place paper liners in 12 mini muffin cups; place a slice of dough in each cup. Bake at 325 degrees for 10 to 12 minutes, or until dough has spread to edges of cups. Beat together cream cheese, condensed milk, egg and vanilla in a medium bowl until smooth. Spoon about 3 tablespoons cream cheese mixture into each cookie cup. Bake for an additional 15 to 18 minutes, or until set. Let cool completely on a wire rack. Carefully remove cups from muffin tin. If desired, top with pie filling. Refrigerate for one hour before serving. Makes one dozen.

Festive...fast! Arrange cookies on a platter, then cover with colorful plastic wrap. It comes in lots of designs and is so simple. Just criss-cross two long sheets of plastic, set the platter in the middle and gather the ends together. Tie it all up with ribbon, and it's ready in no time!

Cheesecake Squares

Jeanne Berfiend
Indianapolis, IN

So quick & easy...perfect for holiday baking.

2 8-oz. pkgs. cream cheese,
 softened
1 egg yolk
1 t. vanilla extract

1/2 c. sugar
2 8-oz. tubes refrigerated
 crescent rolls

Mix together cream cheese, egg yolk, vanilla and sugar until creamy; set aside. Press one tube of crescent rolls into the bottom of a greased 13"x9" baking pan. Spoon cream cheese mixture over crescent layer; top with remaining crescent rolls. Bake at 350 degrees for 25 minutes. Let cool; cut into 1"x1" squares. Makes 2-1/2 to 3 dozen.

Don't forget the music! There's nothing like cheery music in the background to really get friends & family in the holiday spirit.

Mint Brownies

Beth Powell
Potosi, WI

*When I make these for my husband, I usually end up
only getting a small square...they go fast!*

19-1/2 oz. pkg. dark chocolate
   brownie mix
3-oz. pkg, cream cheese,
   softened
1/2 c. butter, softened

1 T. milk
1/2 t. peppermint extract
3 to 4 drops green food coloring
2 c. powdered sugar
Garnish: chocolate frosting

Prepare brownies according to package directions, using the amount
of eggs for cake-like brownies. Bake in a greased 13"x9" baking pan
according to package directions. Let cool. In a bowl, mix cream cheese
and butter until creamy. Add milk, extract, food coloring and powdered
sugar. Spread on cooled brownies; let mint layer harden. Spread with
chocolate frosting; cut into squares. Makes 2-1/2 to 3 dozen.

*Personalize gift tags to make them really special.
Write names on a pressed leaf using a gold marker,
use a paint pen on a pretty glass ornament, or
pipe frosting on bar cookies or cut-outs.*

Can't-Leave-Alone Bars

Dottie Davis
Honesdale, PA

*One of my favorite recipes my daughter, Michelle, first made.
The name says it all!*

18-1/4 oz. pkg. white cake mix
2 eggs
1/3 c. oil
14-oz. can sweetened
  condensed milk

6-oz. pkg. semi-sweet
  chocolate chips
1/4 c. butter, sliced

Combine dry cake mix, eggs and oil in a bowl; mix well. With floured hands, press two-thirds of mixture into a greased 13"x9" baking pan. Set aside. Combine condensed milk, chocolate chips and butter in a microwave-safe bowl. Microwave, uncovered, on high setting for 45 seconds. Stir; microwave an additional 45 to 60 seconds longer or until chips and butter are melted. Stir until smooth; pour over cake mixture in pan. Drop remaining cake mixture by teaspoonfuls over top. Bake at 350 degrees for 20 to 25 minutes or until light golden. Let cool before cutting into squares. Makes 3 dozen.

Mmm...set a yummy oversize cookie on the top of a teacup filled with warm, spicy tea. The cookie keeps the tea warm and the tea warms up the cookie while it's waiting to be enjoyed.

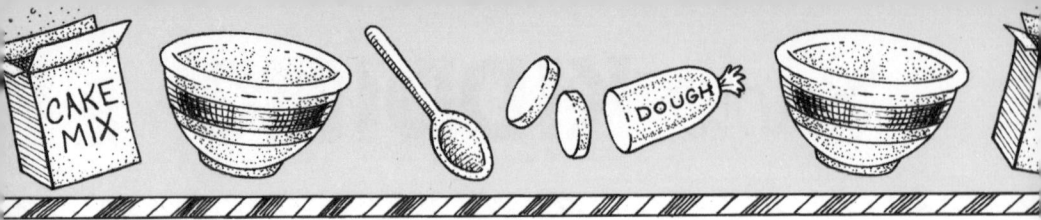

Pinwheel Cake Mix Delights

Dawn Psik
Aliquippa, PA

I LOVE these cookies! So moist and delicious, they're always popular at parties, during the holidays and especially great at bake sales. They go fast!

1/2 c. butter-flavored shortening
1/3 c. plus 1 T. butter, softened
   and divided
2 egg yolks

1/2 t. vanilla extract
18-oz. pkg. fudge marble
   cake mix, divided

Combine shortening, 1/3 cup butter, egg yolks and vanilla in a large bowl. Mix at low speed with an electric mixer until blended. Gradually add dry cake mix to shortening mixture; set aside cocoa packet from cake mix. Blend well. Divide dough into 2 portions. Add cocoa packet and remaining butter to one portion; knead until well blended and chocolate-colored. Roll out yellow dough portion between 2 pieces of wax paper into an 18"x12" rectangle, 1/8-inch thick. Repeat with chocolate dough. Remove wax paper from top of both dough portions; lay yellow dough directly on top of chocolate dough. Remove remaining wax paper; roll up jelly-roll fashion, beginning at long edge. Refrigerate for 2 hours. Cut dough into 1/8-inch slices; place on greased baking sheets. Bake at 350 degrees for 9 to 11 minutes or until lightly golden. Let cool for 5 minutes on baking sheets; remove to wire racks. Makes 3-1/2 dozen.

For a unique shape, lay cookies that are warm from the oven over a rolling pin for 2 minutes or until they take the shape.

Gingerbread Cookies, page 29

Buttermilk Sugar Cookies, page 31

Blonde Brownie Mix in a Jar, page 214

Whoopie Pies, page 56

Icebox Cookies, page 24